The Impact of Organizational Stress on Clinicians

The Impact of Organizational Stress on Clinicians
Professor Bindu Dyna Mason

Published by Spines
ISBN: 979-8-89691-088-6

The Impact of Organizational Stress on Clinicians

Professor Bindu Dyna Mason

Contents

Introduction

The topic of organizational stress among clinicians in healthcare settings is of critical importance. The mental well-being of clinicians has broad implications for care quality, workforce sustainability, patient outcomes, public health, and the moral responsibility to support those who provide care (Ashfaq et al., 2023; Başoğul et al., 2019; Talaee et al., 2020). The impact of organizational stress on the quality of care provided to individuals with mental health issues cannot be overstated. According to LeClaire et al. (2022), when clinicians experience high levels of stress and burnout, their ability to deliver effective care is compromised. This scenario, in turn, can lead to suboptimal outcomes for patients, potentially exacerbating their mental health conditions.

Studies have demonstrated the need for further research in the field of organizational stress management among mental health professionals. For instance, McFadden et al. (2021) and Bruria et al. (2022) needed to demonstrate a better understanding of the effectiveness of stress management within healthcare organizations. They recommended further research to help improve outcomes for both staff and patients, potentially. Similarly, the study by Foster et al. (2018) on mental health nurses' perspectives on a workplace resilience program using a qualitative approach showed a need to examine the topic using an alternative approach and design.

This book aims to create awareness of organizational stress, how clinicians perceive it, and the coping strategies used to manage it.

Background

Mental health clinicians hold a vital role in our healthcare system. They provide essential care and support to individuals with mental health issues (Alderwick & Gottlieb, 2019). Their contribution to the healthcare system is of immense significance, as they are at the forefront of addressing mental health's complex and growing challenges (Ashfaq et al., 2023; Talaee et al., 2020). Başoğul et al. (2019) demonstrated that clinicians are tasked with delivering critical care, therapeutic interventions, and support to individuals struggling with various mental health conditions. Their work goes beyond just providing medical treatment, encompassing empathetic understanding, emotional support, and guidance essential for patients' recovery and overall well-being.

However, they face considerable occupational risks. The risks include challenging work environments and exposure to traumatic conditions, which frequently impact their mental well-being (Yıldırım et al., 2020). The daily experiences of mental health clinicians often bring them into direct contact with distressing and emotionally charged situations. They are exposed to their patients' raw and unfiltered emotions, which can be emotionally draining (Ashfaq et al., 2023). Furthermore, their work environments are often characterized by high-stress levels as they deal with high caseloads and demanding administrative tasks (Yıldırım et al., 2020). These circumstances can place a heavy burden on their mental well-being and overall job satisfaction.

These professionals confront significant challenges related to organizational stress. The challenges stem from factors such as high caseloads, demanding administrative duties, resource limitations, and the emotional toll of their work (Yang & Hayes, 2020; Yıldırım et al., 2020). The demanding nature of their work exposes them to a range of stressors that originate from multiple sources within their professional environment. High caseloads, for instance, require them to manage many cases, each with unique complexities and demands (Yang & Hayes, 2020). This challenge can lead to time pressures and emotional exhaustion as they strive to provide the best care possible to each patient. Demanding administrative tasks adds a layer of stress, as clinicians must handle paperwork, documentation, and bureaucratic responsibilities that can be time-consuming and mentally taxing (Yang & Hayes, 2020). Resource limitations, such as staff shortages or access to necessary equipment, further intensify their stress. These cumulative pressures contribute to emotional exhaustion and the risk of burnout.

Organizational stress could be significantly linked to burnout and secondary trauma among mental health clinicians. The outcome impacts their well-being and the care they deliver (Frieiro Padín et al., 2021; Geisler et al., 2019). The literature demonstrates a significant association between the stress experienced within healthcare organizations and the adverse outcomes of burnout and secondary trauma. For instance, Rollins et al. (2021) claimed that organizational stress was linked to 67% of burnout among mental health clinicians. Burnout is a pervasive issue that affects the mental health of clinicians and their professional performance. It manifests as emotional exhaustion, depersonalization, and reduced personal accomplishment. Clinicians who experience burnout are more likely to exhibit symptoms such as fatigue, reduced motivation, and detachment from their work and patients. Secondary trauma, on the other hand, results from exposure to traumatic narratives and experiences of patients, leading to symptoms similar to those of post-traumatic stress disorder. Understanding and mitigating these outcomes is crucial for the overall well-being of mental health clinicians and the quality of care they provide to patients.

The advent of the COVID-19 pandemic has compounded these stressors. For instance, Holmes et al. (2021) and McFadden et al. (2021) demonstrated that the pandemic brought a unique set of challenges to the field of mental health care, intensifying the existing organizational stressors. Mental health clinicians have witnessed a surge in organizational stress since the pandemic's onset, resulting in increased reports of grief, burnout, and secondary trauma. The pandemic has introduced new dimensions of stress related to the uncertainties, risks, and increased workload imposed by the crisis. The need for remote and telehealth services, the fear of infection, and the emotional toll of dealing with patients' pandemic-related distress have all contributed to heightened stress levels among these professionals. The urgency of understanding how these professionals cope with such stress and trauma has never been more apparent. It is crucial to explore effective coping strategies to provide better support to mental health clinicians during and beyond this challenging period. This study explores and describes the coping strategies these clinicians perceive as effective for managing this stress. This study's findings could help address the organizational stress of clinicians and patients. The findings could also be transferable to other regions within and outside the United States, thereby contributing to improved healthcare workplace practices and outcomes through policy and managerial influence.

Burnout

A state of physical and emotional exhaustion, often accompanied by feelings of detachment and reduced personal accomplishment, resulting from chronic exposure to stress and overwhelming work demands (Talaee et al., 2020)

Coping strategies

Adaptive techniques and behaviors are employed by individuals to manage and mitigate the impact of stress and adversity, promoting psychological well-being and resilience (Buselli et al., 2021). Pahwa & Khan, 2022).

Qualitative descriptive

A qualitative research approach that provides a narrative description of a phenomenon that could be poorly understood in literature(Husserl & Moran, 2012).

Mental Health Clinicians

Professionals in the healthcare sector, including psychologists, psychiatrists, social workers, and counselors, provide care and support to individuals dealing with mental health issues and have issued prescriptions more than 11 times in the past year (Ashfaq et al., 2023).

Optimism

A positive outlook, hope, and confidence in one's ability to navigate difficult situations, even in adversity (Robertson & Cooper, 2013).

Organizational stress

The psychological and emotional strain experienced by individuals within an organization due to various stressors such as high workloads, administrative demands, and resource limitations (Frieiro Padín et al., 2021).

Robertson-Cooper Model of Resilience

A theoretical framework in workplace and organizational studies emphasizes the role of psychological processes, including self-efficacy, optimism, and self-regulation, in fostering individual resilience in challenging work environments (Robertson & Cooper, 2013).

Self-Efficacy

An individual's belief in their capacity to successfully cope with and overcome challenges and adversities in their work environment (Robertson & Cooper, 2013).

Self-Regulation

The ability to effectively manage and control one's emotions, reactions, and behaviors contributes to resilience in the face of workplace stressors (Robertson & Cooper, 2013).

***

The introduction to this study establishes the significance of organizational stress among mental health clinicians in healthcare settings. It underscores these clinicians' crucial role in the healthcare system and their substantial challenges, particularly organizational stress. This stress arises from multiple sources, including high caseloads, demanding administrative tasks, limited resources, and the emotional toll of their work. The COVID-19 pandemic has further intensified these stressors, underscoring the urgency of understanding how clinicians cope with such stress and trauma. The theoretical framework, the Robertson-Cooper Model of Resilience, serves as a core foundation in workplace and organizational studies and aligns with the study's objectives, emphasizing psychological and behavioral elements that promote resilience in the workplace.

The book describes what coping strategies mental health clinicians perceive as effective for managing organizational stress in a healthcare setting. The problem to be addressed in this study is that organizational stress is associated with burnout and secondary trauma among mental health clinicians, but the efficacy of coping mechanisms against such stress and trauma has not been adequately addressed (Frieiro Padín et al., 2021; Geisler et al., 2019). Evidence shows that mental health clinicians have reported increased organizational stress since the COVID-19 pandemic (Holmes et al., 2021). This increased organizational stress contributed to increased mental health clinicians reporting grief, burnout, and secondary trauma since the pandemic (McFadden et al., 2021). This study explores the coping mechanisms mental health clinicians perceive as effective and may provide direction for directors and supervisors to provide instructions on how mental health clinicians manage organizational stress.

A comprehensive literature review on organizational stress and a rigorous and systematic search strategy was developed to access relevant scholarly sources. This strategy involved utilizing a range of reputable library databases and search engines to ensure a thorough exploration of the chosen topic. These databases and search engines were chosen to encompass specialized academic platforms and widely accessible sources, thus facilitating a holistic understanding of Resilience Theory, specifically the Robertson-Cooper Model, and its application within workplace well-being and performance.

Several vital sources were included in the strategy, including library databases and search engines accessed for the literature search. Firstly, PubMed, a renowned biomedical and psychological research database, was employed to identify studies and articles about the psychological facets of resilience and its relevance in the workplace. Secondly, PsycINFO, a premier database for psychological literature, played a pivotal role in uncovering research related to psychological dimensions of workplace resilience and its implications for employee well-being and performance.

To capture inclusivity and a diverse range of sources across various disciplines, Google Scholar, a widely accessible search engine with extensive academic coverage, was also utilized. In addition, EBSCOhost, specifically the Academic Search Premier database, was a valuable resource for identifying scholarly articles related to resilience theory and its applications in the workplace. Lastly, Web of Science, known for its citation indexing and multidisciplinary approach, was instrumental in tracking the citation patterns of seminal works within resilience theory and organizational psychology.

To construct a robust search strategy, careful consideration was given to selecting key search terms that closely align with the focus of this study. The key search terms were resilience theory, medical clinicians, workplace resilience, mental health workers' well-being, mental health, psychological well-being, organizational resilience, resilience interventions, psychological resilience, workplace stress, and Job satisfaction. In addition to these key search terms, Boolean combinations were utilized to refine the search process further and identify the most pertinent sources. These combinations are as follows; "Resilience theory" OR "medical clinics" AND "workplace resilience" OR "mental health workers well-being" OR "mental health worker performance"; "Organizational resilience" OR "resilience interventions" AND "workplace stress" OR "job satisfaction"; "Psychological resilience" OR "resilience theory" AND "employee well-being" OR "employee performance."

Five years (2019–2023) were chosen for source currency and relevancy. Various factors influenced this choice. First, this timeline provides the newest psychology, organizational behavior, management trends, research, and insights. Secondly, it aligns seamlessly with the study's primary goal: to provide insights into contemporary organizational contexts by reflecting on the current realities and challenges organizations and employees face. Lastly, focusing on recent sources enhances the review's academic rigor and quality, as contemporary publications are more likely to have undergone rigorous peer review processes.

The significant sections of the remainder of the chapter will include (a) the Theoretical Framework of the study will be discussed, (b) The relevant studies will then be organized into categories, progressing from the broad subject matter towards the gap to be studied, (c) A conclusion will be given to discuss how the gap was established based on existing literature.

Research has explored how mental health clinicians, including psychologists, psychiatrists, social workers, counselors, and nurses, cause organizational stress. Evidence in the literature supports a successful stress management strategy in this professional group. For instance, Bruria et al. (2022) conducted a qualitative study investigating the strategic stress management of nursing in a changing healthcare sector that creates pressure on nursing administrators and their organizations. The study focused on effective organizational stress management, potentiating quality nursing care, and a two-tiered program to manage organizational stress. The instrument used to measure the interventions' effectiveness indicated a statistically significant decrease in stress-related symptoms among participants. The researchers recommended that in the future, a qualitative study should be done to explore further the long-term effects of these stress management strategies on individual clinicians and the organization. Similarly, McFadden et al. (2021) conducted a qualitative narrative study to understand in-depth knowledge of individual, organizational, and personal perceived effectiveness in managing work-related stress. The study found that stress-inducing management practices included unrealistic demands, lack of support, unfair treatment, low decision latitude, lack of appreciation, imbalance, conflicting roles, lack of transparency, and poor communication. The study recommended that further research investigate developing and implementing comprehensive stress management programs that address these identified stress-inducing factors. In conclusion, the findings of McFadden et al. (2021) and Bruria et al. (2022) highlight how further research assessing the effectiveness of stress management within healthcare organizations can lead to improved outcomes for staff and patients.

The burgeoning field of nursing research sheds light on the pivotal role of coping strategies and resilience-building in managing occupational stress. Researchers in nursing have also explored the role of coping strategies and resilience-building play in managing occupational stress. For instance, Eslami Akbar et al. (2017) conducted a qualitative study with a grounded theory approach to explore the nurses' experiences to reveal the nurses' original coping process when encountering occupational stress. Findings showed that the core variable in the nurse's coping process with job stress was a comprehensive effort to calm stressed conditions. They emphasized that future research should explore the resilience of the coping mechanism in time and if it could be used in other healthcare settings. Similarly, Foster et al. (2018) conducted a qualitative inquiry that explored mental health nurses' perspectives on a workplace resilience program. The study found that mental health nurses were able to strengthen their resilience through understanding resilience and applying cognitive and emotional strategies such as positive self-talk, managing negative self-talk, being aware of and managing emotions, and showing more empathy to address workplace challenges. The researchers recommended that future research determine how resilience-building skills can be incorporated into the day-to-day practice of the nurses as well as the long-term benefit implications for the healthcare practitioners and the healthcare system.

Previous research has also analyzed the experiences of mental health clinicians and their coping strategies in their roles. For instance, Cramer et al. (2020) conducted a quantitative analysis to examine the experiences of mental health clinicians providing services during the COVID-19 pandemic using 161 mental health counselors. The study participants indicated work in private practice settings, community mental health organizations, educational settings, in-patient hospitals, private educational settings, hospice nursing homes, home-based mental health, corrections-based autism clinics, and the Department of Veteran Affairs. The study found that recognizing stressful counseling experiences and learning to respond effectively are critical areas of focus because unmanaged emotional stress responses can increase the risk of empathic occupational hazards, identity confusion, and counselor impairment. Recommendations for future studies included a qualitative methodology to explore whether specific self-care practices, coping responses, or mindfulness practices individually mitigate the effects of perceived stress in a post-pandemic reality and whether differences exist across diverse demographics (e.g., age, race/ethnicity, gender). Similarly, Betke et al. (2021) conducted a qualitative study with 91 nurses in central Poland aged 22–52, describing the relationship between the sense of coherence and coping strategies in a group of professionally active nurses. Findings indicate that nurses from the study group most often declared the use of strategies classified as active ways of coping with stress, focused on the problem. Recommendations for future research were to consider the culture, attitude, and beliefs required to provide in-depth understanding. Both studies highlight the inevitability of the advancement of the studies related to the long-term missions of coping strategies against mental health problems of healthcare professionals.

Further, Joy et al. (2023) conducted a cross-sectional analysis to examine the effect of sources of stress during the peak of the COVID-19 pandemic on nurses´ psychological distress, focusing on the mediating role of coping strategies, both problem-focused and emotion-focused and resilience. Findings show that (a) All the stressors have a significant, direct, and adverse relationship with nurses´ psychological distress; (b) Emotion-focused strategies are negatively related to nurses´ psychological distress directly and indirectly through resilience; and (c) Problem-focused strategies are positively related to nurses´ psychological distress and negatively and indirectly through emotion-focused strategies. Future study recommendations included face-to-face interviews with nurses that allow for obtaining qualitative information. Quantitative studies have been conducted on work-related stress. Chen et al. (2020) used a physiological signal stress level detection scheme and added a physical activity-based context analyzer. The stress detection system that was developed allows users to be aware of their stress levels during their daily activities without creating any interruption or restriction. The only requirement for using this system is to wear a brilliant band. Participants in this study wore the Empatica E4 smart band on their non-dominant hands. The study found that Mindfulness and Yoga were some of the strategies clinicians use to cope with work-related stress. The researchers recommended exploring the potential for these technologies to predict stress-related health outcomes and to facilitate early interventions. In conclusion, these studies highlight the need for future research focused on the long-term effects of continuous stress monitoring on clinicians' mental health and job performance.

Considering the studies that show how effective stress management is in mental health workers, this book can provide insights to help enhance the thickness of contextual and culturally driven stress management and allow for the complementation of the theoretical framework of stress management in healthcare by reinforcing or contradicting existing understanding of stress and coping.

The Robertson-Cooper Model of Resilience serves as a core theoretical framework in workplace and organizational studies. Sir Cary Cooper and Professor Ivan Robertson created this model in 2013, which thoroughly explains how people can manage and adapt to pressures and difficulties at work (Robertson & Cooper, 2013). The model was updated by Shimi and Manwaring (2017). It included the intersections of psychology, sociology, and management, making it a multidisciplinary concept incorporating multiple aspects of human functioning inside businesses. The Robertson Cooper Model of Resilience, developed by Sir Cary Cooper and Professor Ivan Robertson in 2013, has since been a foundational framework in workplace and organizational studies. This model offers valuable insights into individuals' effective management and adaptation to the challenges and pressures encountered in their work environments.

The emphasis on psychological and behavioral elements that promote resilience in the workplace is one of the significant contributions of the Robertson-Cooper Model of Resilience. This paradigm emphasized the importance of psychological processes, including self-efficacy, optimism, and self-regulation, in promoting individual resilience (Robertson & Cooper, 2013). Furthermore, the model emphasized the need for social support within and beyond the business to foster and maintain employee resilience (Pahwa & Khan, 2022). The Robertson-Cooper Model of Resilience implies that encouraging an open communication culture, supporting work-life balance, and giving chances for skill development could all help to improve employee resilience (Robertson & Cooper, 2013). This concept was consistent with Redman's (2005) results, which stressed the importance of organizational tactics targeted at building supportive and caring work environments. By synthesizing these concepts, the Robertson-Cooper model presents a comprehensive perspective on how individuals may effectively cope with adversity, adapt to change, and prosper in challenging organizational contexts.

Chapter 1

Empirical Studies on Resiliency Theory

Several studies have contributed to developing and validating resilience theory, shedding light on its practical applications. As articulated by Hadebe and Ramukumba (2020), resilience theory focuses on the inherent strengths displayed by individuals and systems that empower them to overcome adversity. Instead, the theory highlighted a paradigm shift toward emphasizing individuals' and systems' resilience and capacity in dealing with adversity, as Fahy and Moran (2018) underscored. Research by Pahwa & Khan (2022) emphasized resilience as a dynamic process that could be developed and strengthened rather than a permanent attribute. According to Redman's (2005) study, resilience involved more than just the ability to recover from adversity; it also included the ability to adapt and evolve due to these experiences. This viewpoint emphasizes the need for a comprehensive understanding of resilience, which considers the inherent capabilities of individuals and systems while acknowledging the external supports and resources that assist resilience-building.

The Robertson-Cooper Model of Resilience advances

several significant theoretical premises that offer valuable insights into the concept of resilience. Resilience as a dynamic and evolving process is one of the model's fundamental concepts. Unlike viewing resilience as an innate, fixed attribute, this perspective suggested that individuals and organizations could acquire and cultivate resilience over time (Robertson & Cooper, 2013). Qin and Men (2023) also highlighted the essential elements that influence resilience, which include personality traits, social networks, and workplace factors. The Robertson-Cooper Model further introduced the notion of resilience enhancement, asserting that organizations could use strategies and interventions to bolster resilience at both the individual and organizational levels (Robertson & Cooper, 2013). The Robertson-Cooper Model of Resilience offered a comprehensive framework for understanding and fostering resilience. The theoretical underpinnings of this model emphasize the dynamic nature of resilience acquisition, underscore the critical factors influencing resilience, and advocate for proactive efforts by mental healthcare institutions to enhance resilience among medical clinicians.

Resilience Theory, specifically the Robertson-Cooper Model, has found diverse applications in research and practical contexts, demonstrating its versatility and relevance across various domains. Flint-Taylor et al. (2011) harnessed this theoretical framework to investigate the effects of workplace interventions on the well-being and performance of healthcare practitioners within the National Health Service (NHS). In another scholarly endeavor, the model was employed to probe into the resilience levels among graduate school students, as evidenced in the research conducted by Normand and Anderson (2017). Moreover, the model's utility extended to examining the repercussions of internal communication, particularly during the COVID-19 pandemic, on employee psychological well-being across different levels of interaction, as elucidated in the study by Qin and Men (2023). Collectively, these studies underscore the wide-ranging applicability of the Robertson-Cooper Model in investigating resilience within distinct contexts, from healthcare settings to educational environments and crises.

The selection of Resilience Theory, notably the Robertson-Cooper Model, as the conceptual framework for this study is justified by its direct alignment with the research focus on the well-being and performance of mental health workers within the workplace. Firstly, the Robertson-Cooper Model's emphasis on situational challenges resonates with the core theme of the study, which centers on the workplace environment and the unique stressors encountered by mental health professionals (Robertson & Cooper, 2013). Moreover, the choice of the Robertson-Cooper Model of Resilience as the theoretical foundation for this study is substantiated by its demonstrated applicability in similar contexts. The study of Al Asfoor et al. (2024) was a pertinent example of the model being effectively employed to explore resilience in healthcare systems. The utilization of the Robertson-Cooper Model of Resilience as the theoretical framework for this study is grounded in its unity with the research topic, offering a robust foundation for investigating the coping strategies of mental health clinicians in the face of organizational stress.

The Robertson-Cooper Model's foundation may be vital in understanding the dynamic and adaptive nature of resilience, which is aligned seamlessly with the study's overarching objective, which is to enhance the capacity of mental health clinicians to thrive amidst challenges. There is an inherent suitability of the Robertson-Cooper Model of Resilience to investigate the coping mechanisms adopted by individuals (Robertson & Cooper, 2013). This suitability enables the researchers to explore the coping mechanisms employed by mental health clinicians when facing distinctive stressors within their organizational settings. As elucidated by Robertson and Flint-Taylor (2010), this model provides a solid and well-established conceptual framework, making it particularly apt for this research inquiry. By adopting this theory, the study endeavors to unearth clinicians' precise strategies to bolster their resilience and mitigate the harmful impacts of organizational stress. Therefore, the selection of the Robertson-Cooper Model of Resilience for this study stood as a well-founded choice, offering a robust foundation for exploring how mental health clinicians effectively coped with the difficulties of their profession.

Considering the comprehensive theoretical framework provided above, in the review of the relevant section, the literature relevant to the mental health of medical clinicians will be critically examined, and the contents will be synthesized. In the upcoming section, the researcher delves into a review of relevant literature exploring resilience's diverse facets. While searching and reviewing literature, the researcher will draw insight from studies investigating mental health clinicians' strategies to navigate their unique challenges and promote their resilience.

This section provides a comprehensive contextual backdrop for the study's exploration of coping mechanisms employed by mental health clinicians. This segment serves as an intellectual exploration encompassing several themes, starting with the intricate dynamics of organizational stress and extending to the intricate world of coping strategies, all within the specialized domain of mental health professionals. The objective is to unravel how these clinicians navigate the inherent stressors characterized by their jobs. This inquiry explores how they deal with work-related stress and the caliber of care extended to their clients. This section explores the body of knowledge on organizational stress, the complex world of healthy and unhealthy coping mechanisms, and mental health clinicians' unique difficulties in this setting. It also explores the elements that affect these coping mechanisms' efficacy, with particular attention on the crucial part that self-belief plays in determining how mental health clinicians 'work.

Chapter 2

Organizational Stress

Organizational stress can manifest in various forms, significantly impacting professionals in various fields. With mental health clinicians, this stress was notably characterized by role conflict, role ambiguity, and workload pressure, as discussed in the scholarly literature (Yu et al., 2021). Role conflict emerged when these clinicians found themselves entangled in conflicting demands or expectations within their professional roles, resulting in substantial psychological strain (Gupta & Sahoo, 2020). According to Gupta and Sahoo (2020), this strain was challenging for clinicians to navigate, given that it arose from the incongruence between the idealized roles clinicians were expected to fulfill and the complex realities they encountered in their workplace. In essence, role conflict served as a pivotal facet of organizational stress, shedding light on the intricate dynamics of mental health professionals' experiences within the demanding contexts of their practice (Gupta & Sahoo, 2020; Yu et al., 2021). Such insights underscore the pressing need for developing and implementing effective strategies to mitigate these stressors and enhance the overall well-being of clinicians operating within this vital field.

Workplace stress is a significant issue in mental health care, impacting the well-being of clinicians. Role ambiguity arose when the expectations of a role were unclear or poorly defined, causing uncertainty and stress (Shenoi et al., 2018). Workload pressure involves excessive job demands, such as high caseloads and tight deadlines, which overwhelm clinicians (Scanlan & Still, 2019). These stressors affected individual mental health and had organizational consequences, including reduced job satisfaction and increased turnover rates (Scanlan & Still, 2019). The research conducted by Shenoi et al. (2018) and Scanlan and Still (2019) highlights the tangible impact of role ambiguity and workload pressure on clinicians' mental health in the past. This evidence underscores the importance of addressing these stressors to improve the overall work environment for mental health practitioners.

The prevalence of organizational stress among mental health clinicians has become a growing concern in recent years. A study by Cranage and Foster (2022) emphasized the increasing incidence of organizational stress within the mental health sector, indicating that it has become a pervasive issue that demands attention. Moreover, a comprehensive literature review by Posluns and Gall (2020) found that mental health practitioners had high stress levels primarily due to the inherent stress related to the nature of their work. These findings underscore the gravity of the situation and emphasize the need for comprehensive strategies to address the stressors faced by mental health clinicians in their professional roles. Addressing organizational stress is imperative for the clinicians' well-being and ensuring the delivery of high-quality mental health services to individuals in need.

The emotional strain of dealing with clients with severe

mental health disorders was one of the leading causes of stress among mental health clinicians. Hasan and Tumah (2019) studied how the job's emotional demands, including working with clients with severe mental health disorders, substantially burden mental health practitioners. During the COVID-19 pandemic, stress among mental health clinicians was further exacerbated by administrative responsibilities like paperwork and documentation requirements (Raudenská et al., 2020). The sudden shift to telehealth services and the need for thorough documentation added stress to an already challenging job. The research by Hasan and Tumah (2019) and Raudenská et al. (2020) underscores the multifaceted nature of stress among mental health clinicians, with emotional strain and administrative burdens playing significant roles in the past. Recognizing these sources of stress is crucial for developing effective strategies to support mental health practitioners and enhance their well-being.

Chapter 3

Coping Mechanism and Stressors

Coping mechanisms represent essential cognitive and behavioral strategies individuals employ to manage and navigate various stressors, encompassing internal and external challenges. Algorani and Gupta (2023) have extensively discussed coping mechanisms and their significance in stress management. Additionally, a cross-sectional case-control study conducted by Scanlan and Still (2019) delved into the practical application of these mechanisms, specifically among Turkish nursing students during their ward rounds. The study revealed that coping mechanisms played a pivotal role as adaptive responses to demanding situations, aiding in preserving psychological well-being. In the past, research conducted by Scanlan and Still (2019) shed light on the practical utility of coping mechanisms, demonstrating their positive impact on individuals facing stressors within the healthcare domain. These findings underscore the critical role of coping mechanisms in helping individuals navigate stressful situations effectively. The research by Scanlan and Still (2019) offers a practical perspective, showing that these mechanisms are not merely theoretical concepts but tangible tools that can enhance psychological well-being in real-world scenarios.

The dynamic process of coping mechanisms encompasses individual emotions, behaviors, and thoughts, all working together to address and manage various stressors. This intricate interplay within coping mechanisms was explored in detail by Rossi et al. (2020), emphasizing the multifaceted nature of these strategies. Furthermore, these attributes were found to play a crucial role in stress reduction within the context of mental health practitioners. Research conducted by Hasan and Tumah (2019) demonstrated that these coping mechanisms enhanced problem-solving abilities and regulated emotions among mental health practitioners in the past. The research findings by Rossi et al. (2020) and Hasan and Tumah (2019) emphasize the holistic nature of coping mechanisms involving emotional regulation, cognitive processing, and behavioral responses. However, these studies did not explore the factors essential for developing effective interventions to support mental health professionals in managing their stress and maintaining their well-being.

Understanding how mental health professionals navigate challenging workplace situations is essential, and it involves examining the interplay between these situations and the coping mechanisms they employ. In a qualitative descriptive study conducted by Cranage and Foster (2022), this complex interplay was investigated, shedding light on the strategies employed by mental health nurses. Additionally, Gashi et al. (2022) highlighted the importance of individual emotions and thoughts in enabling mental health clinicians to address their profession's demands effectively. Their research findings provided insights into the integral role of these psychological aspects in coping with the multifaceted challenges faced by mental health professionals. The research conducted by Cranage and Foster (2022) and Gashi et al. (2022) underscores the need for a comprehensive understanding of the coping mechanisms employed by mental health practitioners. It emphasizes that effective coping strategies encompass various cognitive and emotional processes, which can vary among individuals. Recognizing types of coping mechanisms is crucial for tailoring support and interventions to enhance the well-being of mental health clinicians, depending on the mechanism they adopt.

Types of Coping Mechanisms

Coping mechanisms come in various forms, one of which is problem-focused coping, as shown in Figure 1. Altınsoy and Aypay's research in 2023 dived into this specific coping mechanism and its impact on the psychological well-being of mental health nurses. Their study found that problem-focused coping entailed taking direct action to change or eliminate stressors. Mental health clinicians engaged in problem-focused coping by advocating for manageable caseloads or seeking administrative changes to reduce paperwork burdens, as Tsaras et al. (2018) revealed in their past research. The research conducted by Altınsoy and Aypay (2023) and Tsaras et al. (2018) highlights the practicality of problem-focused coping in the mental health field. The evidence from these studies shows that problem-focused coping is proactive, involving actions that can directly address the sources of stress.

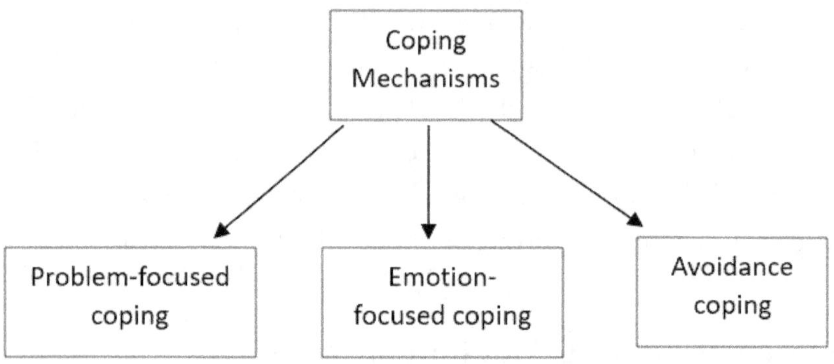

Figure 1. *Types of Coping Mechanisms*

Note. The chart shows three types of coping mechanisms.

Emotion-focused coping is another significant coping mechanism employed by individuals to manage stress. Mefoh et al. (2019) researched to explore the extent to which nursing professionals use emotion-focused coping strategies. Their findings revealed that emotion-focused coping regulates individuals' emotional reactions to stressors. In the mental health field, clinicians commonly utilize emotion-focused coping strategies, such as practicing mindfulness or seeking emotional support from colleagues or supervisors, as identified by Rice et al. (2021). The research by Mefoh et al. (2019) and Rice et al. (2021) underscores the importance of emotion-focused coping in the context of mental health professionals. This coping mechanism allows individuals to address stressors by managing their emotional responses, which can be particularly beneficial in high-stress environments like the mental health field. Although these studies recognize the role of emotion-focused coping, their findings do not emphasize the value of emotional self-care and seeking support from peers and supervisors to enhance well-being.

Another coping mechanism individuals may employ in response to stress is avoidance coping. According to Tahara et al. (2021), avoidance coping refers to a strategy in which an individual deals with stress or problems by attempting to avoid or ignore them rather than confronting them directly. A quantitative cross-sectional study conducted by T. S.-H. Lee et al. (2019) explored the coping mechanisms employed by nurses. They discovered that they often adopted avoidance coping behaviors, which included procrastination, denial, or engaging in distracting activities as a temporary escape from stressors. In a cross-sectional qualitative survey conducted over one week by Tahara et al. (2021), the study analyzed the risk factors and coping mechanisms used by mental healthcare workers in Japan to reduce psychological stress during the COVID-19 pandemic. It was found that mental health clinicians sometimes resorted to avoidance coping strategies when they felt overwhelmed by the emotional intensity of their work. The research findings from T. S.-H. Lee et al. (2019) and Tahara et al. (2021) shed light on the prevalence of avoidance coping mechanisms among healthcare professionals, including mental health clinicians. While these studies show that avoidance coping provides temporary relief from stressors, their methodological approaches were limited to recognizing its potential limitations, as they needed to address the underlying causes of stress. Understanding when and how avoidance coping is employed can inform strategies for promoting more effective and adaptive coping mechanisms among mental health practitioners. Maladaptive and adaptive coping mechanisms will be discussed in detail in the next section on coping strategies.

Chapter 4

Coping Strategies on Employees in General

Corporates have employed Employee Assistance Programs (EAPs) to help their employees cope with work stress and challenges. EAPs are special programs that employers establish for basic supportive services to the staff facing a myriad of personal or professional problems (Brooks & Ling, 2020). EAPs provided workers with the services they needed, comprising psychological counseling, law, and finance consultation, among others, which were targeted at the effective reduction of the stressors (Secapramana et al., 2020). Brooks and Ling (2020) observed that EAPs were significant contributors to the growth and sustainability of business. The researchers found that EAPs helped in reducing stressors from employees' personal and work-related lives so that they can maintain their stability at the place of work and high performance among employees. As Brooks and Ling (2020) and Secapramana et al. (2020) further argue, this was a benefit that did not work for the individual employee but rather improved the general environment of the workplace by cutting down on the possible disturbances emanating from problems related to stress. These studies show that EAPs go beyond individual employee health but also improve employees' organizational resilience and greatly increase productivity.

Companies have also adopted wellness programs to help their employees cope. The approach of wellness programs considers the wide dimension, covering many components that translate into better health outcomes and improved engagement at the workplace when put together. According to Glenn et al. (2022), standard program features in a wellness program for commercial drivers include discounted gym membership, health screenings, nutrition classes, and the provision of facilities or opportunities to engage in competing wellness activities. These components, integrated together, demonstrated a clear and significant reduction in the lost time for health-related absenteeism from the workplace and medical costs by having healthier employees who know how to manage health. Similarly, Björk Brämberg et al. (2021) found that firms that introduced fully developed programs for their staff reported about 30% less use of sick leaves and 25% fewer costs from health insurance. In conclusion, both these studies highlight that the elements associated with two such types of wellness programs not only support the improvements in health status but also contribute to maintaining a more engaged, productive, and financially stable environment for the organization.

Implementation of health and wellness programs across industries bears fruitful results toward employee health, control over stress, and job satisfaction. For instance, Nagler et al. (2021) provided a case study using a multinational corporation that had introduced an efficient wellness program, and found that the job satisfaction of the employees had increased and the complaints related to stress had considerably decreased. Nagler et al. (2021) further found that a properly organized wellness program efficiently resisted both physiological and psychological stressors at the workplace and eventually delivered better, happier, and satisfied employees. Another research by Atoui (2022) investigated a small business that had introduced organized well-being initiatives to its employees and managed to increase the rate of employee retention. The study concluded that these programs were critical not only in big corporations but also in small enterprises. The findings from both of these studies prove that wellness programs have become an integral part of modern business, because they yield benefits that are personal in nature with respect to health and also include enhancements in organizational performance and success in keeping employees.

Although flexible work arrangements have benefits, they also have a fair share of demerits and therefore unique challenges that organizations should effectively manage. The findings of Büssing et al. (2022) showed that less time spent in commuting reduced stress and fatigue; better personal time management, which they then equated to more job satisfaction and job performance. Similarly, the study by Allen (2020) revealed how a technology company, during its transition to the flexible work model, observed decreases in employee stress by 40% and increases in productivity among all employees by 15%. The findings of this study revealed that flexible work, with proper approaches and tools of managing, led to great employee welfare and business results. Similarly, research by Brooks and Ling (2020) showed how a non-profit organization managed to keep the active part of their team's cohesion through using digital collaboration tools, which was a challenging feat in remote work. Such findings by Brooks and Ling (2020) and Allen (2020) show that pro-active communication strategies and pre-planned approaches ensure the positive aspect of enjoying benefits from such flexible arrangements shall not get overpowered by the negative implications, thus fostering efficiency and collaborations at work.

Chapter 5

Coping Mechanisms in Managing Organizational Stress among Healthcare Workers

Coping mechanisms play a vital role in alleviating the immediate effects of stress, offering crucial support to healthcare professionals. Research conducted by Grandinetti et al. (2021) demonstrated how coping mechanisms provided immediate relief from stress by assisting healthcare professionals in regulating their emotional responses and reducing the perceived intensity of stressors, particularly during the first wave of the COVID-19 pandemic. The practical application of coping mechanisms was further highlighted during the pandemic in Italy, as revealed by Rossi et al. (2020). Coping mechanisms served as a lifeline for front-line mental health workers, offering crucial relief from the emotional pressures associated with their employment. Coping mechanisms help regulate emotional responses and improve healthcare professionals' overall well-being (Grandinetti et al., 2021; Rossi et al., 2020). The research by Grandinetti et al. (2021) and Rossi et al. (2020) underscores the immediate and tangible benefits of coping mechanisms in managing organizational stress, particularly in high-stress situations like a global pandemic. Recognizing their role in offering timely relief emphasizes the importance of promoting coping strategies as part of organizational stress management programs in healthcare settings.

Emotion-focused coping mechanisms may efficiently manage emotional discomfort under demanding circumstances, playing a pivotal role in maintaining clinicians' well-being. A qualitative phenomenological study by Scheunemann et al. (2023) delved into the practical effectiveness of emotion-focused coping mechanisms. They found that cognitive reframing and relaxation practices were highly efficient in lowering emotional discomfort among healthcare professionals, particularly when faced with demanding circumstances. In parallel, Wooyoung Kim et al. (2021) discussed the significance of emotion-focused mechanisms, highlighting that they allowed clinicians to regain control and composure during challenging client interactions. Their research emphasized the role of these mechanisms in promoting emotional resilience among healthcare professionals in the past. The findings from Scheunemann et al. (2023) and Wooyoung Kim et al. (2021) emphasize the practical and psychological benefits of emotion-focused coping mechanisms in managing organizational stress. By enabling clinicians to regulate their emotional responses and regain control during challenging situations, these mechanisms contribute significantly to their overall well-being.

Coping methods may also be important in establishing long-term resilience among mental health physicians, allowing them to deal with chronic stresses successfully. An integrated evaluation undertaken by Bui et al. (2023) found that coping methods were influential in developing long-term resilience. According to the findings of this study, mental health nurses who built long-term resilience were better able to overcome adversity and manage well with recurring challenges. Adaptive coping mechanisms, as emphasized by Foster et al. (2019), considerably increased the capacity of mental health practitioners to deal with persistent stress, leading to the development of resilience in the past. Bui et al. (2023) and Foster et al. (2019) did research highlighting the transformational potential of coping strategies in mental health. Although these studies show how coping techniques help with immediate stress alleviation, they do not show how these mechanisms help develop resilience, which mental health physicians need to navigate the chronic obstacles they confront. On the other hand, recognizing the function of coping strategies in long-term resilience highlights their significance as a proactive strategy for boosting the well-being of mental health professionals.

The importance of adaptive coping methods in boosting resilience among persons in high-stress occupations is apparent, especially for mental health providers. Bruria et al. (2022) conducted a study highlighting the importance of adaptive coping methods in improving resilience in high-stress professions. Their findings illuminate how these tactics might successfully equip professionals to handle chronic pressures. Furthermore, Dahan et al. (2022) investigated the resilience of Israeli mental health nurses in qualitative online survey research. According to Dahan et al. (2022), mental health nurses who practice problem-focused coping, seek social support, and practice self-care are more ready to deal with the long-term problems of their careers. These methods helped control acute stress and build resilience. Bruria et al. (2022) and Dahan et al. (2022) did a study highlighting the practical implementation of adaptive coping methods in developing resilience among mental health practitioners.

Coping techniques are essential in reducing the risk of burnout and secondary trauma among mental health providers, providing an essential defense against the negative consequences of persistent stress and emotional depletion. Coping strategies were highlighted as a vital buffer against burnout and secondary trauma in the mental health sector by Delgado et al. (2021), who did a cross-sectional study on the psychological well-being of mental health nurses. This study emphasized the importance of these systems in mitigating the negative repercussions of extended stressor exposure and emotional depletion. The continuous nature of these stresses caused burnout and subsequent trauma, as detailed by Fahy and Moran (2018). Delgado et al. (2021) and Fahy and Moran (2018) study highlights the protective function of coping techniques in the mental health profession. These techniques can minimize the crippling consequences of burnout and secondary trauma by successfully helping physicians manage stress and emotional weariness.

Implementing adaptive coping strategies among clinicians is associated with reduced burnout and secondary trauma, contributing to their overall well-being. A mixed-method survey conducted by Huang et al. (2020) revealed that clinicians who employed adaptive coping strategies, such as reflective practices and self-care routines, were less likely to experience the debilitating effects of burnout and secondary trauma. These strategies empowered them to manage their profession's emotional challenges (Huang et al., 2020). In a quantitative correlational study carried out by Perilli et al. (2022), trait anxiety, stress, and coping mechanisms among frontline healthcare workers were evaluated. The study found that adaptive coping mechanisms played a pivotal role in helping clinicians process their emotions, establish boundaries, and maintain a sense of professional fulfillment. The research conducted by Huang et al. (2020) and Perilli et al. (2022) underscores the practical benefits of adaptive coping mechanisms among mental health clinicians, highlighting the significant role of adaptive coping strategies in mitigating stress-related consequences.

Effective coping methods improve work satisfaction and general well-being among mental health providers. Acker (2018) investigated how good coping improves work satisfaction among mental health practitioners. Coping methods assisted physicians in managing stress and improved their general well-being. Furthermore, Scheepers et al. (2020) discovered that effective coping methods improved the emotional well-being of mental health professionals, increasing their total work satisfaction. In the past, there was a critical relationship between coping techniques and work satisfaction. Acker's (2018) and Scheepers et al.'s (2020) study highlight the practical advantages of suitable coping methods in mental health. Coping methods help doctors deal with stress and contribute to their excellent sentiments about their profession and general well-being. Recognizing the significance of successful coping in improving job satisfaction underlines the relevance of effective coping as a strategy for promoting mental health practitioners' overall health and job satisfaction.

Among mental health doctors, the capacity to successfully manage stress and keep a good attitude at work is highly associated with job satisfaction. Scanlan and Still (2019) performed a study that found a link between the ability to handle stress and maintain a good attitude and work satisfaction in the mental health field. In addition, O'Connor et al. (2018) discovered that physicians using adaptive coping techniques reported better job satisfaction and general well-being. Their research stressed the importance of adaptive coping techniques in increasing work satisfaction and doctors' overall well-being. Effectively managing stress and emotional challenges might help physicians feel more fulfilled in their professions. Scanlan and

Still's (2019) and O'Connor et al.'s (2018) research highlight the critical relationship between coping capacities, work satisfaction, and well-being among mental health physicians. These studies suggest that coping methods are helpful for stress management and contribute to doctors' overall job satisfaction and well-being.

Chapter 6

Adaptive Coping Mechanism

Coping mechanisms used by mental health professionals and nursing students are critical in supporting psychological well-being and positive results. Roca et al. (2021) discovered the importance of adaptive coping techniques in these groups. These processes were distinguished by their potential for long-term psychological well-being and beneficial results. Similarly, adaptive coping methods were critical among professionals working in mental health institutions. Several critical methods were highlighted by Lou et al. (2022), including obtaining social support, participating in self-care routines, and using reflective approaches. These tactics aided clinicians in efficiently managing the demands of their professions. The studies of Roca et al. (2021) and Lou et al. (2022) give essential insights into the adaptive coping methods used by mental health providers and nursing students in the past.

Social Support Systems Among Mental Health Workers

Social support systems, an adaptive coping mechanism, are crucial for reducing psychological stress among mental health workers. A comprehensive review of 44 qualitative and quantitative studies conducted by Yang and Hayes (2020) analyzed the psychological syndrome among psychotherapists. Their findings emphasized the importance of emotional, instrumental, and informational support from various sources in reducing psychological stress among mental health workers. Furthermore, a descriptive analysis of social support's role in mental health among physicians in Iran, conducted by Sun et al. (2020), revealed that various sources of social support systems, such as family, friends, colleagues, and professional networks, played a vital role in helping physicians cope with psychological stress. The research by Yang and Hayes (2020) and Sun et al. (2020) underscores the significance of social support systems in the past by highlighting how support from different sources, including personal and professional networks, contributes to the well-being of mental health workers.

Social support networks are crucial in mitigating stress and improving mental health outcomes among healthcare professionals, particularly during challenging times. During the COVID-19 pandemic, nurses working in mental health wards found solace in their social support networks. Ersin et al. (2022) conducted a study that revealed how these networks acted as a buffer against stress by providing emotional assistance and reducing the perception of stressors. This support played a significant role in helping nurses cope with the unique challenges presented by the pandemic. Furthermore, the research conducted by Kılınç and Sis Çelik (2021) delved into the link between social support and physical health. Their study demonstrated that robust social support systems were associated with better mental and physical health outcomes. The findings from Ersin et al. (2022) underscore the invaluable role of social support networks, particularly during extraordinary circumstances like a pandemic. The emotional assistance and stress reduction provided by these social networks were crucial for the well-being of healthcare professionals (Yang & Hayes, 2020). These findings reaffirm the long-term benefits of robust social support systems in promoting mental and physical health.

Mental health clinicians employ various strategies to cultivate support systems, which are essential for their well-being and effectiveness in their roles. Hou et al. (2020) studied how mental health clinicians actively developed support systems. They utilized strategies such as networking, attending professional conferences, and participating in peer supervision. These activities not only enriched their professional knowledge but also provided them with valuable connections and support. In addition, young Chinese nurses working in clinical settings recognized the importance of maintaining supportive relationships. Chen et al. (2020) found that regularly engaging in team-building activities within clinical settings helped sustain these relationships and provided a robust support system for these nurses. The research by Hou et al. (2020) and Chen et al. (2020) indicates that cultivating support systems through networking, professional engagement, and team-building activities is crucial for their overall well-being and effectiveness in their respective roles. These strategies foster personal and professional growth and contribute to a supportive work environment vital for mental health.

Self-Care Practices Among Mental Health Workers

Self-care techniques are critical for mental health workers to preserve their physical, emotional, and mental well-being and avoid burnout. Mental health practitioners took intentional actions to safeguard their physical, emotional, and mental health to avoid burnout (Monroe et al., 2021). This all-encompassing approach acknowledged the significance of treating all areas of well-being. Joubert and Bhagwan (2018) did an empirical study that shed light on the arduous duties of psychiatric nurses in inpatient mental hospitals. The study indicated an urgent need for mental health practitioners to practice self-care to improve their capacity to offer adequate care. Monroe et al. (2021) previously emphasized the comprehensive aspect of self-care for mental health workers. The researchers stressed the significance of successfully addressing physical, emotional, and mental health issues to prevent burnout. Joubert and Bhagwan (2018) discovered the practical consequences of self-care. Both of these studies show that self-care is good for mental health practitioners' well-being and helps them maintain the quality of treatment they deliver.

Self-care routines are essential to preserving the well-being of people working in therapeutic fields. Jenkins et al. (2019) examined nursing students' self-care responses cross-sectionally. The study found that nursing students who exercised, ate properly, and got adequate sleep had lower stress and better mental health. In a similar vein, Marshman et al.'s systematic review from 2022 highlighted the value of emotional self-care practices within the framework of treatment. The analysis discovered that techniques including journaling, deep breathing exercises, and reaching out for emotional support were essential in reducing the emotional strain of therapeutic work. The studies of Marshman et al. (2022) and Jenkins et al. (2019) offer insightful information on the function of self-care activities in the past. It illustrates how self-care techniques, both mental and physical, are critical for reducing stress and improving psychological health among those who work in therapeutic fields.

Self-care techniques are critical in the field of mental health, acting as a vital buffer against the widespread issue of burnout among mental health caregivers. This assumption is supported by quantitative survey research by La Mott and Martin (2019). Their research looked at the moderating impacts of self-care activities among mental health practitioners, offering insight into how beneficial such practices may be to their overall well-being. According to the findings of this investigation, mental health doctors who engaged in regular self-care routines reported feeling better mentally and physically, lowering their chances of developing burnout. This discovery emphasizes the critical function of self-care as a protective element in the mental health field.

Furthermore, Acker (2018) studied the relationship between self-care behaviors and work satisfaction and underlined the significance of self-care in mental health. According to Acker's research, mental health practitioners who diligently integrated self-care into everyday life had excellent retention and work satisfaction rates. Such empirical data supports the claim that emphasizing self-care activities can protect mental health workers' well-being and contribute to their professions' overall quality and sustainability.

Chapter 7

Maladaptive Coping Mechanism

Maladaptive coping strategies within healthcare, particularly among pre-licensure nursing students and mental health clinicians, have garnered substantial attention in recent research endeavors. Charlton and Wofford's integrative review in 2022 shed light on using maladaptive coping mechanisms by pre-licensure nursing students. They found that while these coping strategies offered a semblance of temporary relief from stress, they ultimately led to detrimental long-term consequences. In a different facet of healthcare, Wilson et al. (2022) undertook a longitudinal analysis to explore moral distress among clinicians in the mental health sector. Contrary to expectations, their study did not uncover maladaptive coping as a predominant response to moral distress. Notably, the average assessments of moral discomfort remained similar between clinicians who could visit patients and those who could not, highlighting the ubiquity of moral distress within the field. These insights underscore the nature of coping mechanisms within healthcare, illuminating the intricate interplay between short-term relief and long-term consequences, as well as the complex dynamics surrounding moral distress among mental health professionals.

Substance Abuse Among Mental Health Practitioners

The intersection of substance abuse, mental health, and professional functioning within the healthcare domain is a critical area of concern. Arble et al.'s (2023) quantitative online survey, focused on nurses in mental health facilities and acute psychiatric wards, unveiled the alarming trend of increased substance abuse among this demographic. The study highlighted that this rise in substance abuse not only heightened the risk of addiction but also resulted in impaired decision-making abilities, ultimately exacerbating the stress levels of these nurses. Such findings underscore the profound impact of substance abuse on the mental health and professional competence of healthcare providers, particularly within specialized mental health settings. Furthermore, the study by Foli et al. (2020), utilizing qualitative content analysis, delved into the intricate relationship between substance use and resilience patterns among nurses in psychiatric wards. Their findings illuminated the harmful consequences of substance abuse, as nurses who engaged in such behavior reported compromised patient care and encountered ethical dilemmas in their professional roles. This collective body of research emphasizes the urgent need for comprehensive interventions and support systems to address substance abuse issues among healthcare professionals, safeguarding their well-being and the quality of care provided to patients in psychiatric settings.

Avoidance and Cognitive-Behaviors Among Mental Health Practitioners

Avoidance behaviors, encompassing actions such as procrastination, withdrawal from work-related responsibilities, and avoidance of challenging conversations, constitute a notable facet of coping mechanisms in various professional contexts. As elucidated by Cain (2019), these behaviors are frequently observed in response to stressors and challenging situations within the workplace. However, it is imperative to consider the long-term consequences of such strategies, as highlighted by Bhandarker and Rai (2019). Their insights emphasized that while avoidance behaviors offered a fleeting sense of relief from immediate stressors, they often perpetuate stress over time. This paradoxical dynamic brought about by these two studies comprehensively highlighted the avoidance behaviors in the workplace and how they inadvertently contribute to a cycle of chronic stress and hinder professional growth and resilience.

Stress, anxiety, and depression among mental health practitioners, particularly those caring for COVID-19-infected patients in psychiatric wards, led them to adopt avoidance coping mechanisms. Salari et al. (2020) conducted a systematic review to approximate the prevalence of these mental health challenges within this specialized healthcare workforce. The review's findings revealed a concerning trend wherein avoidance behaviors, initially providing a semblance of temporary relief from the stressors inherent in their roles, ultimately led to heightened anxiety levels, reduced job satisfaction, and decreased overall productivity among healthcare workers over time. In a parallel context, Elsayed et al. (2018) investigated workplace stress and coping strategies among psychiatric nurses during the pandemic, specifically focusing on the relationship between procrastination and increased stress levels. Their study unveiled that psychiatric nurses who procrastinated responsibilities experienced moderate work-related stress and depression. The collective findings of these studies show the mental health and cognitive challenges mental health practitioners face, particularly during crises like the COVID-19 pandemic.

In response to the formidable challenges presented by the COVID-19 pandemic within mental health wards, Chinese healthcare workers turned to cognitive-behavioral interventions to bolster their resilience and coping mechanisms. Weiner et al. (2020) conducted a quantitative randomized controlled study to evaluate the effectiveness of these interventions, finding that mental health practitioners could effectively confront and overcome avoidance behaviors through online cognitive-behavioral sessions. Meanwhile, Ihara et al. (2023) contributed to understanding cognitive-behavioral interventions through a systematic review, revealing that these approaches primarily focus on reshaping thought patterns and behaviors, often employing techniques like goal setting and time management. Although the impact of cognitive-behavioral therapy on mental health and work performance-related factors was noted to be partial, these findings collectively highlight the potential of cognitive-behavioral interventions in equipping healthcare professionals to navigate the challenges of their roles, particularly amidst unprecedented crises such as the COVID-19 pandemic.

Denial and Suppression Among Mental Health Practitioners

Individuals' use of coping methods such as denial and suppression to address stresses can severely impact their emotional well-being. Denial is the refusal to recognize stress or its emotional consequences, whereas suppression is the purposeful avoidance of emotional expression (Settineri et al., 2019). According to Settineri et al. (2019), individuals use denial and suppression coping methods to deal with stress. However, Cybulska et al. (2022) investigated the effects of emotion suppression on psychological well-being. They found that denial and suppression tactics resulted in emotional problems, such as increased stress, emotional tiredness, and ultimate burnout. Previous study by Settineri et al. (2019) and Cybulska et al. (2022) gives insight into the possible disadvantages of coping methods such as denial and repression. These studies show that while these tactics may provide temporary respite, they can negatively impact emotional well-being and mental health.

Emotion regulation strategies, including mindfulness-based interventions and cognitive-behavioral techniques, may foster healthy emotional processing and expression among mental healthcare workers in China. These tactics have successfully fostered emotional well-being among mental healthcare professionals in China, according to research by Weiner et al. (2020). In particular, cognitive-behavioral methods and mindfulness-based therapies have aided those working in this field learn more efficient ways to manage and communicate their feelings. According to these results, Zhang et al. (2022) emphasized the advantages of cognitive-behavioral methods. According to their research, these strategies helped mental health professionals recognize and productively control their emotions. The investigations by Zhang et al. (2022) and Weiner et al. (2020) provide substantial proof of the advantages of emotion management techniques in the past. These techniques improve mental health professionals' emotional health and capacity to treat patients efficiently.

Resilience Building Techniques

In the crucial self-care arena, resilience-building approaches emerge as another critical component in the repertoire of the mental health therapist. Bastounis et al. (2016) examined the effectiveness of resilience-building activities, particularly emphasizing the Penn Resilience Program. Their investigation found that such programs were very helpful in increasing the resilience of mental health practitioners while simultaneously lowering their stress levels. Furthermore, Vahedi et al. (2016) contributed to this body of information with randomized control research that provided clear evidence that resilience training programs improve psychological resilience. These findings emphasize the importance of resilience-building approaches in preparing mental health practitioners to negotiate their jobs' complicated and emotionally stressful landscape.

The incorporation of mindfulness-based interventions into the realm of mental health care has yielded promising results for the psychological well-being of mental health doctors. Scheepers et al. (2020) comprehensively evaluated how mindfulness techniques like meditation affect clinicians' mental health. According to their extensive investigation, mindfulness-based therapies helped mental health practitioners develop self-awareness and emotional control. Their resilience improved due to increased self-awareness and emotional regulation. Mental health practitioners faced extraordinary obstacles during the COVID-19 epidemic, especially stress. Due to these circumstances, Galbraith et al. (2021) researched qualitative phenomenology on clinical officers' coping techniques in mental health or psychiatric hospitals. Their findings showed that mindfulness-based treatments boosted psychological resilience and reduced stress in these devoted workers (Galbraith et al., 2021; Scheepers et al., 2020). These findings demonstrate the importance of mindfulness techniques in strengthening the mental health workforce, especially during crises, enabling them to offer excellent treatment while protecting their mental health.

Integrating cognitive-behavioral approaches into mental health can increase the resilience of mental health practitioners. According to Melnyk et al. (2020), problem-solving and cognitive reconfiguration improve resilience. This effectiveness stems from their capacity to alter aberrant cognitive processes and increase the coping abilities of mental health professionals. By addressing and correcting problematic thought patterns, cognitive-behavioral approaches assist mental health practitioners in overcoming their various issues. Through their randomized control study on cognitive-behavioral therapies for healthcare worker resilience, Sampson et al. (2019) presented supportive evidence. These findings highlight the relevance of cognitive-behavioral approaches in equipping mental health practitioners with the psychological skills they need to succeed in their demanding work while remaining healthy and providing high-quality care.

Chapter 8

Coping Strategies Unique to Mental Health Clinicians

Clinical supervision serves as a valuable coping strategy for mental health clinicians, aiding in the processing of challenging cases and stress management. For example, the research by Babore et al. (2020) examined the significance of clinical supervision and found that clinical supervision provided a structured framework for reflection, feedback, and skill development among mental health clinicians. This structured approach facilitated professional growth and helped clinicians navigate complex cases more effectively (Babore et al., 2020). Similarly, Salari et al. (2020) conducted a study that analyzed how clinical supervision enabled mental health clinicians to cope with psychological stress related to their roles. The study found that the supportive and collaborative nature of clinical supervision provided a safe space for clinicians to address the emotional challenges inherent in their work. The research by Babore et al. (2020) and Salari et al. (2020) demonstrates that clinical supervision offers mental health clinicians a structured framework for skill development and emotional coping, ultimately contributing to their well-being and professional effectiveness.

Clinical supervision encompasses various models, each offering distinct benefits to mental health clinicians. However, challenges such as power dynamics, trust issues, and balancing clinical demands can affect the effectiveness of the supervisory relationship. Research by Rice et al. (2021) revealed the existence of different supervision models, including the developmental, integrative, and psychodynamic models. These models provided clinicians with unique advantages, such as skill development, self-awareness, and holistic approaches to supervision. In parallel, Scheepers et al. (2020) explored the integrative model, which combined multiple approaches to enhance clinical skills and self-awareness among clinicians. This integrative approach was formed to provide a comprehensive framework for professional growth; however, challenges in clinical supervision were identified by Hou et al. (2020. They found that power dynamics, trust issues, and balancing clinical demands impacted the supervisory relationship. The studies conducted by Rice et al. (2021), Scheepers et al. (2020), and Hou et al. (2020) collectively highlight the complexity of clinical supervision. While different models offer valuable benefits, challenges related to power dynamics and trust issues can hinder the process.

Peer support groups have gained recognition for their ability to provide a safe and confidential space for mental health clinicians to come together and discuss their work-related stressors. Gagne et al. (2018) found that peer support groups allowed mental health professionals to share their experiences, challenges, and coping strategies, creating a sense of community and connection. In tandem, studies conducted by Foglesong et al. (2022) delved into the positive impact of peer support on reducing burnout. They found that peer support groups served as a valuable resource, reducing feelings of isolation and promoting emotional well-being among clinicians. The research by Gagne et al. (2018) and Foglesong et al. (2022) shows that peer support groups provide a platform for sharing experiences and contribute significantly to reducing burnout and fostering community among mental health clinicians.

Forming and maintaining effective peer support networks among mental health clinicians necessitate clear guidelines, regular meetings, and opportunities for open communication. Van Hees et al. (2022) examined the essential elements required for establishing and sustaining effective peer support networks among mental health clinicians. The study's results showed that peer support networks fostered ongoing connections and opportunities for open communication where clinicians freely shared their experiences and challenges. Similarly, Charlton and Wofford (2022) found that organizations and professional associations facilitated the establishment of peer support groups. These entities were critical in creating a supportive environment for mental health professionals to connect and engage in peer-driven support. The research by Charlton and Wofford (2022) and Van Hees et al. (2022) shows that clear guidelines, regular meetings, and organizational support are instrumental in ensuring the success of peer support groups.

Reflective practices play a pivotal role in mental health clinicians' self-assessment and continuous learning, involving systematic review and analysis of their clinical experiences, decisions, and emotions. Reflective practice has garnered attention as a valuable self-assessment and learning process among mental health clinicians. According to Cramer et al. (2020), it involves clinicians systematically reviewing and analyzing their experiences, decisions, and emotions in clinical work. Babore et al. (2020) conducted research that underscored the significance of reflective practice. Their findings revealed that reflection enhanced self-awareness, improved decision-making, and promoted continuous learning among clinicians. According to Huang et al. (2020), mental health clinicians incorporate reflection into their daily routines through journaling, peer discussions, or supervision sessions. The research by Cramer et al. (2020), Babore et al. (2020), and Huang et al. (2020) collectively emphasizes the value of reflective practices, contribute to self-awareness and improved decision-making and support the ongoing professional growth and well-being of mental health clinicians.

Factors Influencing Coping Mechanisms among Mental Health Clinicians

Various factors, including individual differences such as personality traits, influence the selection of coping mechanisms. Personality traits play a significant role in shaping coping preferences, as highlighted by Gashi et al. (2022). Their research revealed that extraversion was associated with a tendency to seek social support as a coping mechanism. In contrast, individuals high in neuroticism were more inclined to rely on emotion-focused coping strategies. In contrast, conscientious individuals were naturally drawn to problem-focused coping, aligning with their goal-oriented and structured nature, as Leszko et al. (2020) identified. The findings from Gashi et al. (2022) and Leszko et al. (2020) underscore the influence of individual personality traits on coping choices. Recognizing these associations allows for a more personalized approach to stress management, where individuals can be guided toward coping strategies that align with their inherent traits. The findings from these studies enhance the role of individual differences in coping mechanisms, providing valuable insights into individuals seeking effective coping strategies and professionals offering guidance in this domain.

The nature of stressors encountered by mental health clinicians can significantly influence their choices of coping mechanisms. Lanza et al. (2018) conducted research that shed light on how mental health clinicians tailored their coping mechanisms to align with the specific characteristics of the stressors they faced. Their study revealed the adaptability of clinicians in selecting coping strategies based on the nature and severity of the stressors. Furthermore, a cross-sectional case-control study involving nursing students, as conducted by Karaca et al. (2019), highlighted that healthcare workers tended to employ problem-focused coping when dealing with administrative stressors and emotion-focused coping when confronted with intense client-related stressors. The study found an adaptability in coping choices based on the nature of the stressors among nursing students. This adaptability was critical in recognizing that different stressors may necessitate different coping strategies (Robertson & Cooper, 2013; Scanlan & Still, 2019). These research findings underscore the pragmatic approach of mental health clinicians in selecting coping mechanisms that best suit the specific stressors they encounter and emphasize the need for a diverse coping toolkit and tailored interventions to address the multifaceted challenges faced by mental health professionals effectively.

The availability of coping resources can considerably influence people's decisions when choosing coping techniques. S. E. Taylor and Stanton (2007) studied coping resources for psychiatric care providers, stressing the impact of the availability or lack of coping resources on coping options. Despite the study's methodological limitations as a review study, it emphasized the necessity of coping resources. Furthermore, Chatterjee et al. (2019) found that access to diverse resources, such as dedicated time for self-care and mental health assistance, was critical in helping healthcare personnel to develop adaptive coping techniques. In contrast, the lack of these resources resulted in using maladaptive coping techniques. The findings of Chatterjee et al. (2019) and S. E. Taylor and Stanton (2007) highlight the importance of coping resources in affecting the coping decisions of healthcare workers.

Developing coping abilities throughout time is critical in determining people's coping mechanism choices. Patel et al. (2021) did studies emphasizing the development of coping skills. Their research found that mental health therapists who developed a repertoire of coping skills via training and experience were better able to choose and apply effective coping strategies. Furthermore, Ee et al. (2020) found that doctors who had gained coping skills over time were better at making informed decisions regarding coping strategies. The research findings of Patel et al. (2021) and Ee et al. (2020) highlight the relevance of continuing skill development in mental health by indicating that coping abilities are not static; they grow and improve with time and experience. These findings show that mental health therapists who invest in refining their coping skills are better prepared to deal with their job's various problems.

Factors Contributing to Coping Strategy Efficacy among Mental Health Clinicians

Various factors influence the effectiveness of coping strategies employed by mental health clinicians. Individual differences play a crucial role in shaping the efficacy of coping strategies. For instance, a study by Louwen et al. (2023) found that mental healthcare worker's personality, cognitive style, and emotional intelligence impacted their choice and effectiveness of coping mechanisms. As indicated earlier, these differences caused clinicians to gravitate toward specific coping strategies based on their unique traits and abilities (Ee et al., 2020; Patel et al., 2021). Furthermore, Başoğul et al. (2019) found that health workers in psychiatric wards with solid emotional intelligence demonstrated the ability to effectively control their reactions to adverse situations. The authors concluded that emotional intelligence was a contributing factor in the successful application of coping strategies among healthcare professionals. The research by Louwen et al. (2023) and Başoğul et al. (2019) shows that individual differences, including personality, cognitive style, and emotional intelligence, influenced the effectiveness of coping strategies among mental health clinicians in the past.

Personal strengths and weaknesses may be pivotal factors in shaping the efficacy of coping strategies employed by individuals. As Louwen et al. (2023) revealed, recognizing one's strengths and weaknesses is critical to effectively managing stress and adversity. Their research elucidated the importance of this self-awareness in selecting coping strategies that were better aligned with an individual's unique characteristics and circumstances. Complementing this perspective, a study conducted by Foster et al. (2019) provided valuable insights into the relationship between emotional strengths and coping strategy adaptability. Their findings suggested that individuals with specific emotional strengths, such as resilience, exhibited a greater capacity to adapt their coping strategies to suit the demands of different situations. These results highlight the interplay between an individual's inherent emotional resources and ability to navigate challenges effectively.

The impact of strong social support networks on the efficacy of coping mechanisms may be a crucial component of resilience and overall health. Van Hees et al. (2022) found that having robust social support networks that include friends, family, and coworkers significantly increased the effectiveness of coping mechanisms. These support networks provided beneficial types of assistance, such as counsel, emotional validation, and access to necessary resources, all of which helped an individual navigate and handle obstacles and pressures better. Moreover, a cross-sectional quantitative investigation by Delgado et al. (2021) confirmed the protective role of a robust social support network against stress. Their results demonstrated how these systems functioned as buffers, assisting people in lessening the damaging effects of stresses on their mental and emotional health. This body of research emphasizes the importance of building and sustaining strong social support networks as a critical element of coping and resilience, especially in the face of professional challenges faced by mental health clinicians.

The development of coping abilities through training and skill development may be critical to the efficient use of coping strategies, especially in the demanding setting of the mental health profession. Bastounis et al. (2016) emphasized the necessity of stress management, communication, and emotional regulation training programs. According to their findings, such training increased the efficacy of coping methods among mental health practitioners. These training efforts enabled clinicians to manage their responsibilities with more resilience and emotional competence by providing them with particular skills and approaches to the issues they confront (Bastounis et al., 2016). Similarly, research by Ee et al. (2020) found that education and skill-building programs strengthened physicians' capacity to cope with job stress and their competence and self-confidence in efficiently managing stress. This collection of research emphasizes that continual education and skill development provide mental health professionals with the skills and information they need to improve their coping strategies, strengthening their well-being and professional efficacy.

Self-awareness and flexibility are critical components in improving the efficiency of coping techniques, especially in the dynamic field of mental health treatment. Scheepers et al. (2020) stressed the critical significance of self-awareness in determining when coping techniques are practical and when modifications are required. This increased self-awareness allowed mental health practitioners to make educated assessments of the appropriateness of their selected coping techniques in response to changing situations and pressures. Foster et al. (2018) performed qualitative inquiry research that explored the perspectives of mental health nurses working within a mental healthcare unit. Their study highlighted the significance of flexibility in the coping process by allowing doctors to adjust their coping strategies flexibly in response to the ever-changing dynamics of their clinical setting. The results of these studies show that the ability to adapt and customize coping techniques to healthcare worker conditions increases the capability of mental health professionals to effectively manage stresses and obstacles in their area, eventually adding to their general well-being and professional competence.

Chapter 9

Self-Belief and Coping

Self-belief plays a significant role in shaping an individual's coping strategies. Self-confidence influences coping. Self-belief develops through personal experiences, social interactions, and cognitive processes. Magli et al. (2020) found self-belief development complicated. Personal accomplishments, failures, and difficulties shape individuals' self-worth and talents. Joy et al. (2023) discovered that cultural background, attributes, and objectives affect self-belief. The culture and society in which people live might affect their self-image and coping skills. Personal attributes and aspirations can also affect self-confidence and coping mechanisms. Magli et al. (2020) and Joy et al. (2023) demonstrate the complexity of self-belief formation and its impact on coping techniques.

Individuals' development of self-belief may be impacted by their own experiences and different interacting elements, notably in the setting of mental health practitioners. According to Magli et al. (2020), self-belief emerged through a complex combination of personal experiences, social relationships, and cognitive processes. These characteristics all contributed to mental health practitioners' perceptions of their strengths and resilience, impacting their attitude toward dealing with the problems of their jobs. In a similar spirit, Chung et al.'s (2021) retrospective study examined the complex character of self-belief among mental health doctors and found that contextual elements, such as cultural context, as well as individual attributes and aspirations, were vital in building self-belief within this unique professional setting. The results of Chung et al. (2021) and Magli et al. (2020) emphasize the complex interplay of personal experiences and external in influencing the development of self-belief among mental health practitioners, ultimately shedding light on the nuances of their coping strategies and ability to provide adequate care in diverse cultural and individual contexts.

Past experiences, feedback, and self-perception may contribute to an individual's self-belief, influencing coping techniques.

Various factors impacted the formation of self-belief, including prior experiences and feedback from others. Keyworth et al. (2019) conducted a qualitative interview study that examined the factors contributing to psychiatric ward nurses' coping mechanisms and found that past successes and failures, as well as feedback received from colleagues and supervisors, significantly contributed to an individual's self-belief. Positive experiences and constructive feedback boosted self-efficacy, reinforcing an individual's belief in their capabilities. Conversely, repeated failures or negative feedback could diminish self-belief (Terry & Newham, 2020). Such experiences may erode an individual's confidence and self-perception, ultimately influencing coping strategies. The research by Keyworth et al. (2019) and Terry and Newham (2020) underscore the dynamic nature of self-belief development. Positive and negative past events and input from others all have a role in molding an individual's self-perception and coping techniques.

Role of Self-Belief in Coping with Organizational Stress

Self-belief is crucial in motivating mental healthcare workers to engage proactively in coping strategies, ultimately influencing their ability to navigate workplace challenges effectively. Nawal et al. (2022) discovered that mental health professionals were driven by their beliefs. Their self-assurance encouraged them to employ coping mechanisms actively. Additionally, optimism aids in overcoming adversity. Self-efficacy, or the firm conviction that one can overcome obstacles at work, is developed by mental health physicians who have confidence in themselves (Wu et al., 2022). Similarly, Delgado et al. (2021) found a connection between mental health nurses' resilience and self-belief. According to their research, nurses with strong self-esteem were better able to handle stress and maintain their well-being. According to studies by Nawal et al. (2022), Wu et al. (2022), and Delgado et al. (2021), coping methods used by mental healthcare workers are motivated by their self-belief. These studies highlight that mental health professionals with self-confidence are more likely to be resilient and able to overcome challenges since they are actively encouraged to experiment with and employ coping mechanisms.

Self-belief may also influence the utilization of coping strategies among mental health workers, particularly during challenging circumstances like the COVID-19 pandemic. A study conducted by Joy et al. (2023) examined the self-esteem and psychological resilience of mental health workers in Qatar during the COVID-19 pandemic and found that staff nurses who strongly believed in their abilities were more likely to persist in seeking and applying effective coping mechanisms. Similarly, Rose and Smith (2018) conducted research that assessed the role of self-belief in goal setting and achievement among Australian healthcare workers, including mental health clinicians. Their study revealed that mental health clinicians with strong self-belief were better equipped to set specific, challenging coping-related goals and work diligently toward their successful attainment. The research by Joy et al. (2023) and Rose and Smith (2018) demonstrates how self-belief influences motivation and facilitates the strategic planning and implementation of coping strategies.

Self-belief indeed holds a significant role in evaluating one's coping abilities and strategies, especially within the context of healthcare workers, particularly in mental healthcare settings. Labrague's (2021) systematic review found a connection between self-belief and how healthcare workers in the mental healthcare field perceived their coping abilities. Individuals with higher levels of self-belief had a more positive appraisal of their coping skills, as Joy et al. (2023) corroborated. The researchers concluded that positive self-perception instilled greater confidence in their capacity to effectively manage the stressors inherent in their roles. The results of Labrague (2021) and Joy et al. (2023) illustrate that self-belief catalyzes bolstering resilience and enhancing the overall well-being of healthcare workers, as it encourages a proactive approach to stress management and a more constructive outlook on their ability to navigate the unique challenges within mental healthcare settings.

Interventions focusing on self-awareness can serve as transformative tools in redirecting self-belief towards healthier and more effective coping strategies, particularly within mental healthcare's challenging and stressful context. Joy et al. (2023) analyzed the relationship between self-awareness and self-regulation therapies and how they influenced a shift of self-belief toward healthier coping strategies. These therapies helped mental health workers understand their coping strategies, identify their strengths and shortcomings, and make better stress management decisions. For instance, cognitive restructuring, as demonstrated by Nawal et al. (2022), was employed to challenge and correct erroneous assumptions regarding the efficacy of various coping strategies among mental healthcare workers. This process helped individuals reframe their beliefs, leading to a more adaptive and resourceful approach to coping. Chung et al.'s (2021) findings further underscored the positive outcomes of strengthening self-belief in healthcare professionals, as it was linked to reduced stress levels and increased job satisfaction. These collective insights emphasize the transformative potential of self-awareness interventions in reshaping self-belief, ultimately promoting healthier coping strategies and enhancing the well-being of those working in the demanding mental healthcare field.

Recent advancements in data collection techniques have expanded the scope and depth of empirical research. For example, a more detailed quantitative analysis, like that of Cramer et al. (2020), stretched the experiences of mental health counselors during COVID-19 to emphasize further the different settings for their practice, such as private practice and the Department of Veterans Affairs. A range of sources for data such as those outlined would enable researchers to gain a depth and breadth of insights that would be sensitive to the complexity of analysis between demographics and environments. The research proved the fact that the research must have the proper instruments, sources, and references relevant to the objectives for making the data collection exact and reasonable. Another example is the study by Perilli et al. (2022), in which the source data were self-reported and aimed to reveal mechanisms between the sense of coherence and the coping strategies among nurses. In so doing, the tools helped in capturing personal and emotional responses that are not easily quantified by such physiological measures, hence giving an overall view of the psychological effects of stress and subjective efficacy in relation to the various coping mechanisms.

Mental health professionals use interviews and focus groups to investigate the experience and perception of organizational stress. For instance, in their empirical research, Keyworth et al. (2019 collected data through in-depth interviews with the nurses to determine how they cope with their process of encountering job-related stress. The findings were organized from personal strategies to organizational challenges. Accordingly, Foster et al. (2018) conducted focused group interviews in their study to capture the fine-tuned aspects of what mental health nurses felt towards the perspective of resilience programs in the workplace. This is an inductive, informative design for unmasking the complex dynamics of stress and coping in the healthcare environment, thus allowing the researcher entry into the nuance of the interplay between individual coping mechanisms and organizational culture. Detailed qualitative data that will be collected will help establish effective interventions for management with context specificity, which would form a part of organizational policies and practices.

Integrating electronic health records in the research process gives a comprehensive perspective of stress management interventions comprising all-time periods. Recent studies, for example, by Yang and Hayes (2020), followed longitudinally the performance of resilience training over time among youth and emergent adulthood populations with mental disorders using health records. Further research was done by Patel et al. (2021) on using electronic health records to determine the long-lasting effects of practicing stress reduction techniques in clinical patients. Using digital health records to provide longitudinal data enables researchers to observe changes that take place over long periods. Observing the interventions and individual coping strategies also contributed to a dynamic view of the long-term impacts. This approach cements the research findings on the sustainability of developing mental health practices and policies supporting ongoing well-being among health professionals. Organizational stress, a burning problem in the context of mental health care, is one of the contributing factors to the phenomenon of burnout and secondary trauma among mental health professionals (Frieiro Padín et al., 2021; Geisler et al., 2019). The strain of management workload in the healthcare system has worsened with the advent of the COVID-19 pandemic, as healthcare workers reported spikes in organizational stress (Holmes et al., 2021). Stress levels have gone up to the extent of secondary trauma, grief, and burnout among mental health care professionals, and there is an increase in the number of reports on this. However, these experts' stress management tactics for organizational stress do not portray its essence. Nevertheless, they have great significance because they can be used to make more accurate decisions by management officials who may have a choice to make to improve employee support (Magli et al., 2020). Such studies reflect that uncovering mental health professionals' coping mechanisms and resilience tactics is of significant concern for creating a complex support system. Precise measures focusing on clinicians' specific problems in crises like the COVID-19 pandemic can cushion the administration.

Organizational stress may have far-reaching consequences, notably contributing to burnout in the mental health sector. Foster et al. (2019) conducted a comprehensive study that linked organizational stress to burnout among mental health practitioners. As identified by emotional exhaustion, depersonalization, and reduced personal accomplishment, burnout was a significant concern. Additionally, research by Shenoi et al. (2018) found that mental health clinicians experiencing high levels of burnout in the past were more likely to consider leaving their profession. This connection between burnout and attrition highlighted the urgency of addressing burnout in the mental health field. The findings from Foster et al. (2019) and Shenoi et al. (2018) demonstrate the dire consequences of burnout in the mental health sector, leading to potential workforce shortages and diminished quality of care. Recognizing the role of organizational stress in burnout underscores the need for systemic changes and support mechanisms to combat this issue effectively.

Exposure to clients' traumatic experiences posed a significant risk of secondary trauma among mental health clinicians, which includes vicarious trauma or compassion fatigue, and had profound emotional and psychological effects on these professionals. Research conducted by J. J. Lee et al. (2018) delved into the impact of secondary trauma on mental health clinicians, shedding light on the emotional and psychological toll it exacted. Additionally, a cross-sectional quantitative study by Kobayashi et al. (2020) explored the concept of secondary trauma, specifically in mental health nurses in Japan, providing further insights into the prevalence and effects of this phenomenon in a different cultural context. These studies collectively underscored the global concern surrounding secondary trauma among mental health professionals in the past. The research by J. J. Lee et al. (2018) and Kobayashi et al. (2020) highlights the significance of addressing secondary trauma in the mental health field and the universal importance of implementing strategies to mitigate its impact on clinicians' well-being.

Research has also highlighted the work-related stressors faced by midwives and nurses. Favrod et al. (2018) used a mixed-method approach to investigate nurses' specific stressors, highlighting the emotionally taxing nature of their work. The study showed that a significant aspect of nurses' mental health challenges involved dealing with grief and loss, which impacted clinicians personally and professionally. In parallel, research conducted by Rabow et al. (2021) delved into the experiences of grief among healthcare professionals, revealing that grief-related stressors such as the loss of clients, the emotional burden of witnessing client suffering, and the cumulative effect of multiple losses significantly impacted the mental health of nurses. The findings from Favrod et al. (2018) and Rabow et al. (2021) emphasize the unique challenges nurses and other healthcare professionals face when dealing with grief and loss in their line of work. However, they still need to assess further the importance of providing support and resources to help clinicians cope with these emotionally demanding aspects of their profession. The following section delves into literature that explores the coping mechanisms used by clinicians to cope with emotionally demanding aspects of their profession.

Individual differences, including personal preferences for problem-focused or emotion-focused coping strategies, can significantly influence the selection of coping mechanisms. Wu et al. (2020) conducted a cross-sectional quantitative study that explored psychological resilience and coping strategies among undergraduate clinical students within an acute mental health ward. Their research revealed that coping styles were individualized coping response patterns that varied among mental health clinicians, highlighting the influence of individual differences. Additionally, research by Terry and Newham (2020) suggested that individual medical practitioners preferred either problem-focused or emotion-focused coping, influenced by past experiences and coping efficacy. These preferences played a crucial role in determining the coping mechanisms selected when dealing with organizational stress in the past. These preferences were shaped by individual experiences and perceptions of coping efficacy, which influenced the selection of coping mechanisms (Terry & Newham, 2020; Wu et al., 2020). The findings from Wu et al. (2020) and Terry and Newham (2020) underscore the importance of recognizing the diversity of coping preferences among mental health clinicians.

The organizational context, including workplace culture and norms, can influence the choice of coping mechanisms among mental health workers. Research conducted by Desai et al. (2021) highlighted the substantial impact of organizational culture and norms on the selection of coping mechanisms. The researchers found that within mental health organizations, the workplace culture and norms significantly shaped clinicians' health workers' strategies. A supportive and open organizational culture encouraged mental health clinicians to seek help and engage in adaptive coping strategies, as observed in the study by Lokko et al. (2016). Conversely, a toxic or stigmatizing culture within the organization led to adopting avoidance coping mechanisms to respond to stress. These studies' findings agreed that a positive and supportive organizational culture fostered adaptive coping strategies and encouraged help-seeking behaviors. Conversely, a hostile or stigmatizing culture may hinder the adoption of effective coping mechanisms, leading to less constructive approaches (Algorani & Gupta, 2023; Galbraith et al. (2021). The research findings from Desai et al. (2021) and Lokko et al. (2016) emphasize the critical role of organizational context in determining the coping mechanisms employed by mental health clinicians.

Organizational context, including the presence of support systems within the organization, can significantly guide the choices of coping mechanisms among mental health clinicians. Van Hees et al. (2022) conducted research that underscored the role of supportive supervisors and peer networks in guiding the coping choices of mental health clinicians. Their study demonstrated that these support systems within the organization substantially impacted clinicians' coping decisions. Additionally, research by Foglesong et al. (2022) emphasized the importance of leadership and peer support in promoting adaptive coping strategies among healthcare workers. Clinicians who perceived their supervisors and colleagues as sources of support were more likely to adopt effective coping strategies, as evidenced by the study conducted by Shalaby and Agyapong (2020). Although these authors recognized the influence of organizational support systems, their research did not highlight their importance in promoting the well-being of mental health professionals and facilitating effective stress management. However, the findings from Van Hees et al. (2022), Foglesong et al. (2022), and Shalaby and Agyapong (2020) highlight the critical role of support systems within the organization in shaping the coping choices of mental health clinicians. These findings show that the presence of supportive supervisors and peer networks encourages the adoption of adaptive coping mechanisms among mental health workers and fosters a sense of trust and connection within the workplace.

Summary

The literature examination revealed three key themes involving coping techniques among mental health clinicians who face organizational stress. One recurring theme is the presence of significant organizational stressors within the mental health profession, such as role conflict, role ambiguity, and workload pressure, all of which have a significant impact on clinicians' well-being at work (Scanlan & Still, 2019; Shenoi et al., 2018; Yu et al., 2021). This collection of research emphasizes the mental health profession's complex nature and the critical need for appropriate coping methods to handle these stresses.

Another prominent theme centers on the importance of adaptive coping strategies in mitigating the adverse effects of organizational stress. The literature underscores the value of strategies such as seeking social support, engaging in self-care practices, utilizing reflective techniques, and employing cognitive-behavioral approaches to manage and navigate stress effectively (Joy et al., 2023; Labrague, 2021; Melnyk et al., 2020; Roca et al., 2021). These adaptive mechanisms enhance individual well-being and contribute to the overall resilience of mental health clinicians. Conversely, maladaptive coping strategies, including substance abuse and avoidance behaviors, have been identified as harmful responses to stressors with long-term negative consequences, highlighting the critical importance of adopting adaptive approaches (Arble et al., 2023; Cain, 2019; Charlton & Wofford, 2022).

Additionally, the literature reveals that mental health clinicians employ coping strategies unique to their profession, such as clinical supervision, peer support groups, and reflective practices, to navigate the distinct challenges they encounter effectively (Babore et al., 2020; Cramer et al., 2020; Foglesong et al., 2022). These specialized coping mechanisms highlight the significance of peer and professional support networks within the mental health field. Furthermore, self-belief, encompassing self-esteem and self-confidence, emerges as a pivotal theme in influencing how mental health clinicians cope with organizational stress. High self-belief is associated with better-coping strategies and resilience, emphasizing the interconnectedness of psychological factors with coping mechanisms (Joy et al., 2023; Magli et al., 2020; Wu et al., 2022).

Organizational stress finds substantial support in the literature, emphasizing the importance of both adaptive (Joy et al., 2023; Labrague, 2021; Melnyk et al., 2020; Roca et al., 2021) and maladaptive coping mechanisms (Arble et al., 2023; Cain, 2019; Charlton & Wofford, 2022). The self-belief of mental health clinicians is firmly rooted in the literature's recurring theme of self-belief's role in influencing coping strategies and resilience, which is shaped by personal experiences and environmental factors (Delgado et al., 2021; Joy et al., 2023; Magli et al., 2020; Wu et al., 2022). The more extensive talks about self-belief necessarily include components of self-esteem, which provides valuable background for possible implications for self-esteem in the context of mental health professionals (Joy et al., 2023; Nawal et al., 2022; Wu et al., 2022). In summary, the literature contextualizes thoroughly and emphasizes the link between coping methods, self-belief, and their possible effect on self-esteem among mental health clinicians.

This book makes a substantive contribution to the existing literature by addressing identified gaps through an in-depth exploration of the intricate relationship between self-belief and coping strategies among mental health clinicians in the context of organizational stress. To give a thorough knowledge of coping processes within this professional sector, this research intends to explore the complex dynamics of how personal experiences create self-belief and, in turn, impact the selection and efficacy of coping methods.

Bibliography

Acker, G. M. (2018). Self–care practices among social workers: Do they predict job satisfaction and turnover intention? Social Work in Mental Health, 16(6), 713–727. https://doi.org/10.1080/15332985.2018.1494082

Adler, R. H. (2022). Trustworthiness in qualitative research. Journal of Human Lactation: Official Journal of International Lactation Consultant Association, 38(4), 598–602. https://doi.org/10.1177/08903344221116620

Adu, P., & Miles, D. A. (2023). Dissertation research methods: A step-by-step guide to writing up your research in the social sciences. Taylor & Francis.

Al Asfoor, D., Tabche, C., Al-Zadjali, M., Mataria, A., Saikat, S., & Rawaf, S. (2024). Concept analysis of health system resilience. Health Research Policy and Systems, 22(1), 43. https://doi.org/10.1186/s12961-024-01114-w

Alderwick, H., & Gottlieb, L. M. (2019). Meanings and misunderstandings: A social determinants of health lexicon for health care systems. >The Milbank Quarterly, 97(2), 407. https://doi.org/10.1111%2F1468-0009.12390

Algorani, E. B., & Gupta, V. (2023). Coping mechanisms. StatPearls Publishing. http://www.ncbi.nlm.nih.gov/books/NBK559031/

Alhazmi, A. A., & Kaufmann, A. (2022). Phenomenological qualitative methods analyze cross-cultural experiences in novel educational and social contexts. Frontiers in Psychology, 13, 785134. https://doi.org/10.3389/fpsyg.2022.785134

Allen, C. K. (2020). The relationship of individual employee attributes and generational association in a multicultural, multigenerational, high-tech, American work environment (Publication No. 28154477) [Published doctoral dissertation, Northcentral University]. ProQuest.

Altınsoy, F., & Aypay, A. (2023). A post-traumatic growth model: Psychological hardiness, happiness-increasing strategies, and problem-focused coping. Current Psychology, 42>(3), 2208–2220. https://doi.org/10.1007/s12144-021-02466-0

Andrade, C. (2021). The inconvenient truth about convenience and purposive samples. Indian Journal of Psychological Medicine, 43(1), 86–88. https://doi.org/10.1177/0253717620977000

Arble, E., Manning, D., Arnetz, B. B., & Arnetz, J. E. (2023). Increased substance use among nurses during the COVID-19 Pandemic. International

Journal of Environmental Research and Public Health, 20(3), 2674. https://doi.org/10.3390/ijerph20032674

Ashfaq, F., Abid, G., Ilyas, S., & Mansoor, K. B. (2023). Perceived organizational support and work engagement among health sector workers during the COVID-19 pandemic: a multicentre, time-lagged, cross-sectional study among clinical hospital staff in Pakistan. BMJ Open, 13(6), e065678. http://dx.doi.org/10.1136/bmjopen-2022-065678

Atoui, R. (2022). Leadership effectiveness and its impact on employee engagement, productivity, and sustainability in small businesses: A quantitative study(Publication No. 29397386) [Published doctoral dissertation, Northcentral University]. ProQuest.

Babore, A., Lombardi, L., Viceconti, M. L., Pignataro, S., Marino, V., Crudele, M., Candelori, C., Bramanti, S. M., & Trumello, C. (2020). Psychological effects of the COVID-2019 pandemic: Perceived stress and coping strategies among healthcare professionals. Psychiatry Research, 293, 113366. https://doi.org/10.1016/j.psychres.2020.113366

Barroga, E., Matanguihan, G. J., Furuta, A., Arima, M., Tsuchiya, S., Kawahara, C., Takamiya, Y., & Izumi, M. (2023). Conducting and writing quantitative and qualitative research. Journal of Korean Medical Science, 38(37), e291. https://doi.org/10.3346/jkms.2023.38.e291

Başoğul, C., Arabacı, L. B., Büyükbayram, A., Aktaş, Y., & Uzunoğlu, G. (2019). Emotional intelligence and personality characteristics of psychiatric nurses and their situations of exposure to violence. Perspectives in Psychiatric Care, 55(2), 255–261. https://doi.org/10.1111/ppc.12358

Bastounis, A., Callaghan, P., Banerjee, A., & Michail, M. (2016). The effectiveness of the Penn Resiliency Programme (PRP) and its adapted versions in reducing depression and anxiety and improving explanatory style: A systematic review and meta-analysis. Journal of Adolescence, 52, 37–48. https://doi.org/10.1016/j.adolescence.2016.07.004

Bayot, M. L., Brannan, G. D., Brannan, G. D., Brannan, J. M., & Tenny, S. (2023). Human subjects research design. StatPearls.

Betke, K., Basińska, M. A., & Andruszkiewicz, A. (2021). Sense of coherence and strategies for coping with stress among nurses. BMC Nursing, 20(1), 107.

Bevens, W., Reece, J., Jelinek, P. L., Weiland, T. J., Nag, N., Simpson-Yap, S., Gray, K., Jelinek, G. A., & Neate, S. L. (2022). The feasibility of an online educational lifestyle program for people with multiple sclerosis: A qualitative analysis of participant semi-structured interviews. Digital Health, 8, 20552076221123713. https://doi.org/10.1177/20552076221123713

Bhandarker, A., & Rai, S. (2019). Toxic leadership: Emotional distress and coping strategy. Internahttps://doi.org/10.1108/IJOTB-03-2018-0027

Bhangu, S., Provost, F., & Caduff, C. (2023). Introduction to qualitative research methods - Part I. Perspectives in Clinical Research, 14(1), 39–42. https://doi.org/10.4103/picr.picr_253_22

Björk Brämberg, E., Arapovic-Johansson, B., Bültmann, U., Svedberg, P., & Bergström, G. (2021). Prevention of sick leave at the workplace: design of a cluster-randomized controlled trial of a problem-solving intervention among employees with common mental disorders. BMC Public Health, 21, 1-13.

Borgstede, M., & Scholz, M. (2021). Quantitative and qualitative approaches to generalization and replication - A representationalist view. Frontiers in Psychology, 12, 605191. https://doi.org/10.3389/fpsyg.2021.605191

Braun, V., & Clarke, V. (2021). Thematic analysis. In E. Lyons & A. Coyle (Eds.) Analysing qualitative data in psychology(pp. 128-147).Sage Publications.

Braun, V., & Clarke, V. (2021). To saturate or not to saturate? Questioning data saturation as a useful concept for thematic analysis and sample-size rationales. Qualitative Research in Sport, Exercise and Health, 13(2), 201-216. https://doi.org/10.1080/2159676X.2019.1704846

Brooks, C. D., & Ling, J. (2020). "Are we doing enough?": An examination of the utilization of employee assistance programs to support the mental health needs of employees during the COVID-19 pandemic. Journal of Insurance Regulation, 39(8).

Bruria, A., Maya, S.-T., Gadi, S., & Orna, T. (2022). Impact of emergencies on resilience at work and burnout of Hospital's healthcare personnel. International Journal of Disaster Risk Reduction, 76, 102994. https://doi.org/10.1016/j.ijdrr.2022.102994

Buetow, S., & Zawaly, K. (2022). Rethinking researcher bias in health research. Journal of Evaluation in Clinical Practice</em>, 28m>(5), 843–846. https://doi.org/10.1111/jep.13622

Bui, M. V., McInnes, E., Ennis, G., & Foster, K. (2023). Resilience and mental health nursing: An integrative review of updated evidence. International Journal of Mental Health Nursing, 32(4), 1055–1071. https://doi.org/10.1111/inm.13132

Buselli, R., Corsi, M., Veltri, A., Baldanzi, S., Chiumiento, M., Del Lupo, E., & Cristaudo, A. (2021). Mental health of health care workers (HCWs): A review of organizational interventions put in place by local institutions to cope with new psychosocial challenges resulting from COVID-19. Psychiatry Research</em>, (299), 1138-47. https://doi.org/10.1016/j.psychres.2021.113847

Büssing, A., Zupanic, M., Ehlers, J. P., & Taetz-Harrer, A. (2022). Mental stress in medical students during the pandemic and their relation to digital and hybrid semester—cross-sectional data from three recruitment waves in Germany. International Journal of Environmental Research and Public Health, 19(17), 11098.

Cain, C. K. (2019). Avoidance problems reconsidered. Current Opinion in Behavioral Sciences, 26, 9–17. https://doi.org/10.1016/j.cobeha.2018.09.002

Charlton, A. C., & Wofford, L. G. (2022). Maladaptive coping behaviors in pre-licensure nursing students: An integrative review. Journal of Professional Nursing, 39,> 156–164. https://doi.org/10.1016/j.profnurs.2022.01.011

Chatterjee, D., Chopra Chatterjee, S., & Bhattacharyya, T. (2019). Exploring self-care abilities among women in prisons of West Bengal, India. International Journal of Prisoner Health, 16(2), 185–198. https://doi.org/10.1108/IJPH-04-2019-0025

Chen, J., Li, J., Cao, B., Wang, F., Luo, L., & Xu, J. (2020). Mediating effects of self-efficacy, coping, burnout, and social support between job stress and mental health among young Chinese nurses. Journal of Advanced Nursing, 76(1), 163–173. https://doi.org/10.1111/jan.14208

Chung, J., Lobbezoo, F., van Selms, M. K. A., Chattrattrai, T., Aarab, G., & Mitrirattanakul, S. (2021). Physical, psychological, and sociodemographic predictors relate to patients' self-belief in the etiology of temporomandibular disorders. Journal of Oral Rehabilitation, 48(2), 109–123. https://doi.org/10.1111/joor.13113

Clair, C. A., Melvin, T. J., Taylor, J. L., & Saylor, M. A. (2022). "Researcher" bias: How our assumptions on technology affect research of older adults. Frontiers in Public Health, 10, 1034497. https://doi.org/10.3389/fpubh.2022.1034497

Cleland, J., MacLeod, A., & Ellaway, R. H. (2021). The curious case of case study research. Medical Education, 55(10), 1131–1141. https://doi.org/10.1111/medu.14544

Cramer, R. J., Ireland, J. L., Hartley, V., Long, M. M., Ireland, C. A., & Wilkins, T. (2020). Coping, mental health, and subjective well-being among mental health staff in secure forensic psychiatric settings: Results from a workplace health assessment. Psychological Services, 17(2), 160–169. https://doi.org/10.1037/ser0000354

Cranage, K., & Foster, K. (2022). A qualitative descriptive study of mental health nurses' experience of challenging workplace situations. International Journal of Mental Health Nursing, 31(3), 665–676.

Cranage, K., & Foster, K. (2022). Mental health nurses' experience of challenging workplace situations: A qualitative descriptive study.

International Journal of Mental Health Nursing, 31(3), 665–676. https://doi.org/10.1111/inm.12986

Cybulska, A. M., Rachubińska, K., Stanisławska, M., Grochans, S., Cymbaluk-Płoska, A., & Grochans, E. (2022). Analysis of factors related to mental health, suppression of emotions, and personality influencing coping with stress among nurses. International Journal of Environmental Research and Public Health, 19(16), Article 16. https://doi.org/10.3390/ijerph19169777

Dahan, S., Levi, G., & Segev, R. (2022). Shared trauma during the COVID-19 pandemic: Psychological effects on Israeli mental health nurses. International Journal of Mental Health Nursing, 31(3), 722–730. https://doi.org/10.1111/inm.12996

Daraz, L., & Bouseh, S. (2021). Developing a quality benchmark for determining the credibility of web health information- a protocol of a gold standard approach. Frontiers in Digital Health, 3, 801204. https://doi.org/10.3389/fdgth.2021.801204

Delgado, C., Roche, M., Fethney, J., & Foster, K. (2021). Mental health nurses' psychological well-being, mental distress, and workplace resilience: A cross-sectional survey. International Journal of Mental Health Nursing, 30(5), 1234–1247. https://doi.org/10.1111/inm.12874

Denieffe, S. (2020). Commentary: Purposive sampling: complex or simple? Research case examples. Journal of Research in Nursing: JRN, 25(8), 662–663. https://doi.org/10.1177/1744987120928156

Desai, M. U., Paranamana, N., Restrepo-Toro, M., O'Connell, M., Davidson, L., & Stanhope, V. (2021). Implicit organizational bias: Mental health treatment culture and norms as barriers to engaging with diversity. American Psychologist, 76(1), 78–90. https://doi.org/10.1037/amp0000621

Dosek, T. (2021). Snowball sampling and Facebook: How social media can help access hard-to-reach populations. PS: Political Science & Politics, 54(4), 651–655. doi:10.1017/S1049096521000041X

Doyle, L., McCabe, C., Keogh, B., Brady, A., & McCann, M. (2020). An overview of the qualitative descriptive design within nursing research. Journal of Research in Nursing: JRN, 25(5), 443–455. https://doi.org/10.1177/1744987119880234

Ee, C., Lake, J., Firth, J., Hargraves, F., de Manincor, M., Meade, T., Marx, W., & Sarris, J. (2020). An integrative, collaborative care model for people with mental illness and physical comorbidities. International Journal of Mental Health Systems, 14(1), 83. https://doi.org/10.1186/s13033-020-00410-6

Elsayed, S., Hasan, A. A., & Musleh, M. (2018). Work stress, coping strategies and levels of depression among nurses working in mental health hospital in

Port-Said city. International Journal of Culture and Mental Health, 11(2), 157–170. https://doi.org/10.1080/17542863.2017.1343859

Elstad, E. A., Lutfey, K. E., Marceau, L. D., Campbell, S. M., von dem Knesebeck, O., & McKinlay, J. B. (2010). What do physicians gain (and lose) with experience? Qualitative results from a cross-national study of diabetes. Social Science & Medicine (1982), 70(11), 1728–1736. https://doi.org/10.1016/j.socscimed.2010.02.014

Ersin, F., Havlioğlu, S., & Gür, S. C. (2022). Mental well-being and social support perceptions of nurses working in a Covid-19 pandemic hospital. Perspectives in Psychiatric Care, 58(1), 124–131. https://doi.org/10.1111/ppc.12833

Eslami Akbar, R., Elahi, N., Mohammadi, E., & Fallahi Khoshknab, M. (2017). How do the nurses cope with job stress? A study with grounded theory approach. Journal of Caring Sciences, 6(3), 199–211. https://doi.org/10.15171/jcs.2017.020

Fahy, G., & Moran, L. (2018). Who supports the psychiatric nurse? A qualitative study of the social supports that affect how psychiatric nurses cope with workplace risks and stressors. Irish Journal of Sociology, 26(3), 244–266. https://doi.org/10.1177/0791603518792366

Favrod, C., Jan du Chêne, L., Martin Soelch, C., Garthus-Niegel, S., Tolsa, J.-F., Legault, F., Briet, V., & Horsch, A. (2018). Mental health symptoms and work-related stressors in hospital midwives and NICU nurses: A mixed methods study. Frontiers in Psychiatry, 9.https://www.frontiersin.org/articles/10.3389/fpsyt.2018.00364

Flint-Taylor, J., Durose, J., & Wigley, C. (2011). Keeping pressure positive: Improving well-being and performance in the NHS through innovative leadership development. In I. Robertson & C. Cooper (Eds.), Well-being: productivity and happiness at work (pp. 193–202). Palgrave Macmillan UK. https://doi.org/10.1057/9780230306738_18

Foglesong, D., Spagnolo, A. B., Cronise, R., Forbes, J., Swarbrick, P., Edwards, J. P., & Pratt, C. (2022). Perceptions of supervisors of Peer Support Workers (PSW) in behavioral health: Results from a national survey. Community Mental Health Journal, 58(3), 437–443. https://doi.org/10.1007/s10597-021-00837-2

Foli, K. J., Reddick, B., Zhang, L., & Krcelich, K. (2020). Substance use in registered nurses: "I heard about a nurse who . . ." Journal of the American Psychiatric Nurses Association, 26(1), 65–76. https://doi.org/10.1177/1078390319886369

Foster, K., Cuzzillo, C., & Furness, T. (2018). Strengthening mental health nurses' resilience through a workplace resilience program: A qualitative inquiry. Journal of Psychiatric and Mental Health Nursing, 25(5–6), 338–348. https://doi.org/10.1111/jpm.12467

Foster, K., Roche, M., Delgado, C., Cuzzillo, C., Giandinoto, J.-A., & Furness, T. (2019). Resilience and mental health nursing: An integrative review of international literature. International Journal of Mental Health Nursing, 28(1), 71–85. https://doi.org/10.1111/inm.12548

Frieiro Padín, P., Verde-Diego, C., Arias, T. F., & González-Rodríguez, R. (2021). Burnout in health social work: An international systematic review (2000–2020). European Journal of Social Work, 24(6), 1051–1065. https://doi.org/10.1080/13691457.2020.1870215

Gagne, C. A., Finch, W. L., Myrick, K. J., & Davis, L. M. (2018). Peer workers in the behavioral and integrated health workforce: Opportunities and future directions. American Journal of Preventive Medicine, 54(6, Supplement 3), S258–S266. https://doi.org/10.1016/j.amepre.2018.03.010

Galbraith, N., Boyda, D., McFeeters, D., & Hassan, T. (2021). The mental health of doctors during the COVID-19 pandemic. BJPsych Bulletin, 45(2), 93–97. https://doi.org/10.1192/bjb.2020.44

Gashi, D., Gallopeni, F., Imeri, G., Shahini, M., & Bahtiri, S. (2022). The relationship between Big Five personality traits, coping strategies, and emotional problems through the COVID-19 pandemic. Current Psychology</em>. https://doi.org/10.1007/s12144-022-03944-9

Geisler, M., Berthelsen, H., & Muhonen, T. (2019). Retaining social workers: The role of quality of work and psychosocial safety climate for work engagement, job satisfaction, and organizational commitment. Human Service Organizations: Management, Leadership & Governance, 43(1), 1–15. https://doi.org/10.1080/23303131.2019.1569574

George Washington University. (2022). HealthLandscape - Turning statistics into information. GW. https://maps.healthlandscape.org/GW/

Glenn, T. L., Mabry, J. E., & Hickman, J. S. (2022). A catalogue of health and wellness programs for commercial drivers.

Gomez-Diaz, T., & Recio, T. (2022). Research software vs. research data I: Towards a research data definition in the open science context. F1000Research, 11, 118. https://doi.org/10.12688/f1000research.78195.2

Grandinetti, P., Gooney, M., Scheibein, F., Testa, R., Ruggieri, G., Tondo, P., Corona, A., Boi, G., Floris, L., Profeta, V. F., G. Wells, J. S., & De Berardis, D. (2021). Stress and maladaptive coping of Italian health care professionals during the first wave of the pandemic. Brain Sciences, 11(12). https://doi.org/10.3390/brainsci11121586

Green, J., Hanckel, B., Petticrew, M., Paparini, S., & Shaw, S. (2022). Case study research and causal inference. >BMC Medical Research

Methodology, 22(1), 307. https://doi.org/10.1186/s12874-022-01790-8

Griffith, D. M., Jaeger, E. C., Bergner, E. M., Stallings, S., & Wilkins, C. H. (2020). Determinants of trustworthiness to conduct medical research: Findings from focus groups conducted with racially and ethnically diverse adults. Journal of General Internal Medicine, 35(10), 2969–2975. https://doi.org/10.1007/s11606-020-05868-1

Gupta, S., & Sahoo, S. (2020). Pandemic and mental health of the front-line healthcare workers: A review and implications in the Indian context amidst COVID-19. General Psychiatry, 33(5), e100284. https://doi.org/10.1136/gpsych-2020-100284

Hadebe, N. K. F., & Ramukumba, T. S. (2020). Resilience and social support of young adults living with mental illness in the city of Tshwane, Gauteng province, South Africa. Curationis, 43(1), 1-7. http://dx.doi.org/10.4102/curationis.v43i1.2084

Hasan, A. A., & Tumah, H. (2019). The correlation between occupational stress, coping strategies, and the levels of psychological distress among nurses working in a mental health hospital in Jordan. Perspectives in Psychiatric Care, 55(2), 153–160. https://doi.org/10.1111/ppc.12292

Hasbrouck, M. A., & Waddimba, A. C. (2017). The work-related stressors and coping strategies of group-employed rural health care practitioners: A qualitative study. American Journal of Industrial Medicine, 60(10), 867–878. https://doi.org/10.1002/ajim.22753

Holmes, M. R., Rentrope, C. R., Korsch-Williams, A., & King, J. A. (2021). Impact of COVID-19 pandemic on posttraumatic stress, grief, burnout, and secondary trauma of social workers in the United States. Clinical Social Work Journal, 49(4), 495–504. https://doi.org/10.1007/s10615-021-00795-y

Hou, T., Zhang, T., Cai, W., Song, X., Chen, A., Deng, G., & Ni, C. (2020). Social support and mental health among health care workers during Coronavirus Disease 2019 outbreak: A moderated mediation model. PLoS One, 15(5), e0233831. https://doi.org/10.1371/journal.pone.0233831

https://www.bls.gov/spotlight/2023/healthcare-occupations-in-2022/home.htm

Huang, L., Lei, W., Xu, F., Liu, H., & Yu, L. (2020). Emotional responses and coping strategies in nurses and nursing students during Covid-19 outbreak: A comparative study. PLoS OneE, 15(8), e0237303. https://doi.org/10.1371/journal.pone.0237303

Hudon, C., Chouinard, M. C., Bisson, M., Danish, A., Karam, M., Girard, A., Bossé, P. L., & Lambert, M. (2021). Case study with a participatory approach: Rethinking pragmatics of stakeholder engagement for implementation research. Annals of Family Medicine, 19(6), 540–546. https://doi.org/10.1370/afm.2717

Husserl, E., & Moran, D. (2012). Ideas: General introduction to pure phenomenology. Routledge.

Ihara, Y., Kurosawa, T., Matsumoto, T., & Takizawa, R. (2023). The effectiveness of preventive group cognitive-behavioral interventions on enhancing work performance-related factors and mental health of workers: A systematic review. Current Psychology, 42(4), 2797–2810. https://doi.org/10.1007/s12144-021-01562-5

Jenkins, E. K., Slemon, A., O'Flynn-Magee, K., & Mahy, J. (2019). Exploring the implications of a self-care assignment to foster undergraduate nursing student mental health: Findings from a survey research study. Nurse Education Today, 81, 13–18. https://doi.org/10.1016/j.nedt.2019.06.009

Jenkins, S. P., Calvert, M. J., & Draper, H. (2020). Potential research participants' use of information during the consent process: A qualitative pilot study of patients enrolled in a clinical trial. PloS One, 15(6), e0234388. https://doi.org/10.1371/journal.pone.0234388

Johnson, J. L., Adkins, D., & Chauvin, S. (2020). A review of the quality indicators of rigor in qualitative research. American Journal of Pharmaceutical Education, 84(1), 7120. https://doi.org/10.5688/ajpe7120

Joubert, P. D., & Bhagwan, R. (2018). An empirical study of the challenging roles of psychiatric nurses at in-patient psychiatric facilities and its implications for nursing education. International Journal of Africa Nursing Sciences, 9, 49–56. https://doi.org/10.1016/j.ijans.2018.08.001

Jowsey, T., Deng, C., & Weller, J. (2021). General-purpose thematic analysis: a useful qualitative method for anaesthesia research. BJA Education, 21(12), 472–478. https://doi.org/10.1016/j.bjae.2021.07.006

Joy, G. V., Alomari, A. M. A., Singh, K., Hassan, N., Mannethodi, K., Kunjavara, J., & Al Lenjawi, B. (2023). Nurses' self-esteem, self-compassion, and psychological resilience during the COVID-19 pandemic. Nursing Open, 10(7), 4404–4412. https://doi.org/10.1002/nop2.1682

Kajamaa, A., Mattick, K., & de la Croix, A. (2020). How to … do mixed-methods research. The Clinical Teacher, 17(3), 267–271. https://doi.org/10.1111/tct.13145

Karaca, A., Yildirim, N., Cangur, S., Acikgoz, F., & Akkus, D. (2019). Relationship between mental health of nursing students and coping, self-esteem and social support. Nurse Education Today, 76, 44–50. https://doi.org/10.1016/j.nedt.2019.01.029

Keyworth, C., Epton, T., Goldthorpe, J., Calam, R., & Armitage, C. J. (2019). 'It is difficult, I think it is complicated': Health care professionals' barriers and enablers to providing opportunistic behavior change interventions during routine medical consultations. British Journal of Health Psychology, 24(3), 571–592. https://doi.org/10.1111/bjhp.12368

Kılınç, T., & Sis Çelik, A. (2021). Relationship between the social support and psychological resilience levels perceived by nurses during the COVID-19 pandemic: A study from Turkey. Perspectives in Psychiatric Care, 57(3), 1000–1008. https://doi.org/10.1111/ppc.12648

Kimak, A., & Woźniacka, A. (2023). How old is too old to work for physicians?. Postepy Dermatologii i Alergologii, 40(3), 368–371. https://doi.org/10.5114/ada.2023.128977

Kobayashi, Y., Oe, M., Ishida, T., Matsuoka, M., Chiba, H., & Uchimura, N. (2020). Workplace Violence and Its Effects on Burnout and Secondary Traumatic Stress among Mental Healthcare Nurses in Japan. International Journal of Environmental Research and Public Health, 17(8). https://doi.org/10.3390/ijerph17082747

Koka, K. M., Yadlapalli, S., Pillarisetti, P., Yasangi, M. K., Yaragani, A., & Kummamuru, S. (2021). The barriers for tobacco cessation counseling in teaching health care institutions: A qualitative data analysis using MAXQDA software. Journal of Family Medicine and Primary Care, 10(9), 3262–3267. https://doi.org/10.4103/jfmpc.jfmpc_19_21

Labrague, L. J. (2021). Psychological resilience, coping behaviors, and social support among health care workers during the COVID-19 pandemic: A systematic review of quantitative studies. Journal of Nursing Management, 29(7), 1893–1905. https://doi.org/10.1111/jonm.13336

La Mott, J., & Martin, L. A. (2019). Adverse childhood experiences, self-care, and compassion outcomes in mental health providers working with trauma. Journal of Clinical Psychology, 75(6), 1066–1083. https://doi.org/10.1002/jclp.22752

Lanza, A., Roysircar, G., & Rodgers, S. (2018). First responder mental healthcare: Evidence-based prevention, postvention, and treatment. Professional Psychology: Research and Practice, 49(3), 193–204. https://doi.org/10.1037/pro0000192

LeClaire, M., Poplau, S., Linzer, M., Brown, R., & Sinsky, C. (2022). Compromised integrity, burnout, and intent to leave the job in critical care nurses and physicians. Critical Care Explorations, 4(2). https://doi.org/10.1097%2FCCE.0000000000000629

Lee, J. J., Gottfried, R., & Bride, B. E. (2018). Exposure to client trauma, secondary traumatic stress, and the health of clinical social workers: A mediation analysis. Clinical Social Work Journal, 46(3), 228–235. https://doi.org/10.1007/s10615-017-0638-1

Lee, T. S.-H., Tzeng, W.-C., & Chiang, H.-H. (2019). Impact of coping strategies on nurses' well-being and practice. Journal of Nursing Scholarship, 51(2), 195–204. https://doi.org/10.1111/jnu.12467

Leszko, M., Iwański, R., & Jarzębińska, A. (2020). The relationship between personality traits and coping styles among first-time and recurrent prisoners in Poland. Frontiers in Psychology, 10. https://www.frontiersin.org/articles/10.3389/fpsyg.2019.02969

Litam, S. D. A., Ausloos, C. D., & Harrichand, J. J. S. (2021). Stress and resilience among professional counselors during the COVID-19 pandemic. Journal of Counseling and Development: JCD, 99(4), 384–395. https://doi.org/10.1002/jcad.12391

Lokko, H. N., Chen, J. A., Parekh, R. I., & Stern, T. A. (2016). Racial and ethnic diversity in the US psychiatric workforce: A perspective and recommendations. Academic Psychiatry, 40(6), 898–904. https://doi.org/10.1007/s40596-016-0591-2

Lorente, L., Vera, M., & Peiró, T. (2021). Nurses' stressors and psychological distress during the COVID-19 pandemic: The mediating role of coping and resilience. Journal of Advanced Nursing, 77(3), 1335–1344. https://doi.org/10.1111/jan.14695

Lou, N. M., Montreuil, T., Feldman, L. S., Fried, G. M., Lavoie-Tremblay, M., Bhanji, F., Kennedy, H., Kaneva, P., & Harley, J. M. (2022). Nurses' and physicians' distress, burnout, and coping strategies during COVID-19: Stress and impact on perceived performance and intentions to quit. Journal of Continuing Education in the Health Professions, 42(1), e44. https://doi.org/10.1097/CEH.0000000000000365

Louwen, C., Reidlinger, D., & Milne, N. (2023). Profiling health professionals' personality traits, behavior styles, and emotional intelligence: A systematic review. BMC Medical Education, 23(1), 120. https://doi.org/10.1186/s12909-023-04003-y

Magli, A. S., Sabri, M. F., & Rahim, H. A. (2020). The influence of financial attitude, financial behavior, and self-belief towards financial vulnerability among public employees in Malaysia. Malaysian Journal of Consumer and Family Economics, 25, 175–193.

Marshman, C., Hansen, A., & Munro, I. (2022). Compassion fatigue in mental health nurses: A systematic review. Journal of Psychiatric and Mental Health Nursing, 29(4), 529–543. https://doi.org/10.1111/jpm.12812

Mbidoaka, K. C. (2017). Strategies to reduce effects of organizational stress in health care workplaces (Publication No. 5414) [Published doctoral dissertation, Walden University]. ScholarWorks.

Mbuagbaw, L., Lawson, D. O., Puljak, L., Allison, D. B., & Thabane, L. (2020).

A tutorial on methodological studies: The what, when, how and why. BMC Medical Research Methodology, 20(1). https://doi.org/10.1186/s12874-020-01107-7

McFadden, P., Ross, J., Moriarty, J., Mallett, J., Schroder, H., Ravalier, J., Manthorpe, J., Currie, D., Harron, J., & Gillen, P. (2021). The role of coping in the wellbeing and work-related quality of life of UK health and social care workers during COVID-19. International Journal of Environmental Research and Public Health, 18(2), Article 2. https://doi.org/10.3390/ijerph18020815

Mefoh, P. C., Ude, E. N., & Chukwuorji, J. C. (2019). Age and burnout syndrome in nursing professionals: The moderating role of emotion-focused coping. Psychology, Health & Medicine, 24(1), 101–107. https://doi.org/10.1080/13548506.2018.1502457

Melnyk, B. M., Kelly, S. A., Stephens, J., Dhakal, K., McGovern, C., Tucker, S., Hoying, J., McRae, K., Ault, S., Spurlock, E., & Bird, S. B. (2020). Interventions to improve mental health, well-being, physical health, and lifestyle behaviors in physicians and nurses: A systematic review. American Journal of Health Promotion, 34(8), 929–941. https://doi.org/10.1177/0890117120920451

Monroe, C., Loresto, F., Horton-Deutsch, S., Kleiner, C., Eron, K., Varney, R., & Grimm, S. (2021). The value of intentional self-care practices: The effects of mindfulness on improving job satisfaction, teamwork, and workplace environments. Archives of Psychiatric Nursing, 35(2), 189–194. https://doi.org/10.1016/j.apnu.2020.10.003

Murphy, M., McCaughan, E., Carson, M. A., Donovan, M., Wilson, R. H., & Fitzsimons, D. (2020). Nothing to lose: a grounded theory study of patients' and healthcare professionals' perspectives of being involved in the consent process for oncology trials with non-curative intent. BMC Palliative Care, 19(1). https://doi.org/10.1186/s12904-020-00661-7

Nagai, H., Nakazawa, E., & Akabayashi, A. (2022). The creation of the Belmont Report and its effect on ethical principles: A historical study. Monash Bioethics Review, 40(2), 157–170. https://doi.org/10.1007/s40592-022-00165-5

Nagler, E. M., Stelson, E. A., Karapanos, M., Burke, L., Wallace, L. M., Peters, S. E., Nielsen, K., & Sorensen, G. (2021). Using Total Worker Health® Implementation guidelines to design an organizational intervention for low-wage food service workers: The workplace organizational health study. International Journal of environmental research and public health, 18(17), 9383.

Nawal, A., Shoaib, M., Zámečník, R., & Rehman, A. U. (2022). Effects of occupational stress, self-efficacy, and mental health during the pandemic on hospital sanitation workers in Malaysia. Evaluation & the Health Professions, 45(3), 313–324. https://doi.org/10.1177/01632787221112079

Normand, C., & Anderson, L. (2017). Graduate attributes in higher education: attitudes on attributes from across the disciplines. Taylor & Francis.

Northall, T., Chang, E., Hatcher, D., & Nicholls, D. (2020). The application and tailoring of Colaizzi's phenomenological approach in a hospital setting. Nurse Researcher, 28(2), 20–25. https://doi.org/10.7748/nr.2020.e1700

Nyirenda, L., Kumar, M. B., Theobald, S., Sarker, M., Simwinga, M., Kumwenda, M., Johnson, C., Hatzold, K., Corbett, E. L., Sibanda, E., & Taegtmeyer, M. (2020). Using research networks to generate trustworthy qualitative public health research findings from multiple contexts. >BMC Medical Research Methodology, 20(1), 13. https://doi.org/10.1186/s12874-019-0895-5

Occupational Employment and Wage Statistics. (2020, July 6). U.S. Bureau of Labor Statistics. Retrieved August 5, 2024, from https://www.bls.gov/oes/2019/may/oes291223.htm#nat

O'Connor, K., Neff, D. M., & Pitman, S. (2018). Burnout in mental health professionals: A systematic review and meta-analysis of prevalence and determinants. European Psychiatry, 53,74–99. https://doi.org/10.1016/j.eurpsy.2018.06.003

Öhlén, J., & Friberg, F. (2023). Empirical phenomenological inquiry: Guidance in choosing between different methodologies. Global Qualitative Nursing Research, 10, 23333936231173566. https://doi.org/10.1177/23333936231173566

Opare, F. Y., Aniteye, P., Afaya, A., & Glover-Meni, N. (2020). "We try our best to offer them the little that we can" coping strategies of Ghanaian community psychiatric nurses: a qualitative descriptive study. BMC Nursing, 19(1). https://doi.org/10.1186/s12912-020-00449-3

Pahwa, S., & Khan, N. (2022). Factors affecting emotional resilience in adults. Management and Labour Studies, 47(2), 216-232. https://doi.org/10.1177/0258042X211072935

Patel, M., Swift, S., & Digesu, A. (2021). Mental health among clinicians: What can we know and do? International Urogynecology Journal, 32(5), 1055–1059. https://doi.org/10.1007/s00192-021-04805-y

Peddle, M. (2022). Maintaining reflexivity in qualitative nursing research. Nursing Open, 9(6), 2908–2914. https://doi.org/10.1002/nop2.999

Perilli, E., Perazzini, M., Bontempo, D., Ranieri, F., Di Giacomo, D., Crosti, C., Marcotullio, S., & Cobianchi, S. (2022). Reduced anxiety associated to adaptive and mindful coping strategies in general practitioners compared with hospital nurses in response to covid-19 pandemic primary care reorganization. Frontiers in Psychology, 13, 891470. https://doi.org/10.3389/fpsyg.2022.891470

Portigal, S. (2023). Interviewing users: How to uncover compelling insights. Rosenfeld Media.

Posluns, K., & Gall, T. L. (2020). Dear mental health practitioners, take care of yourselves: A literature review on self-care. International Journal for the Advancement of Counselling, 42(1), 1–20. https://doi.org/10.1007/s10447-019-09382-w

Qin, Y. S., & Men, L. R. (2023). Exploring the impact of internal communication on employee psychological well-being during the COVID-19 Pandemic: The mediating role of employee organizational trust. International Journal of Business Communication, 60(4), 1197–1219. https://doi.org/10.1177/23294884221081838

Rabow, M. W., Huang, C.-H. S., White-Hammond, G. E., & Tucker, R. O. (2021). Witnesses and victims: Healthcare workers and grief in the time of COVID-19. Journal of Pain and Symptom Management, 62(3), 647–656. https://doi.org/10.1016/j.jpainsymman.2021.01.139

Raudenská, J., Steinerová, V., Javůrková, A., Urits, I., Kaye, A. D., Viswanath, O., & Varrassi, G. (2020). Occupational burnout syndrome and post-traumatic stress among healthcare professionals during the novel coronavirus disease 2019 (COVID-19) pandemic. Best Practice & Research Clinical Anaesthesiology, 34(3), 553–560. https://doi.org/10.1016/j.bpa.2020.07.008

Redman, C. L. (2005). Resilience theory in archaeology. American Anthropologist, 107(1), 70–77. https://doi.org/10.1525/aa.2005.107.1.070

Renjith, V., Yesodharan, R., Noronha, J. A., Ladd, E., & George, A. (2021). Qualitative methods in health care research. International Journal of Preventive Medicine</em>, 12, 20. https://doi.org/10.4103/ijpvm.IJPVM_321_19

Rice, K., Rock, A. J., Murrell, E., & Tyson, G. A. (2021). The prevalence of psychological distress in an Australian TAFE sample and the relationships between psychological distress, emotion-focused coping, and academic success. Australian Journal of Psychology, 73(2), 231–242. https://doi.org/10.1080/00049530.2021.1883408

Robertson, I., & Cooper, C. L. (2013). Resilience. Stress and Health: Journal of the International Society for the Investigation of Stress</em>, 29(3), 175–176. https://doi.org/10.1002/smi.2512

Robertson, I., & Flint-Taylor, J. (2010). Wellbeing in healthcare organizations:

Key issues. British Journal of Healthcare Management, 16(1), 18–25. https://doi.org/10.12968/bjhc.2010.16.1.45895

Roca, J., Canet-Vélez, O., Cemeli, T., Lavedán, A., Masot, O., & Botigué, T. (2021). Experiences, emotional responses, and coping skills of nursing students as auxiliary health workers during the peak COVID-19 pandemic: A qualitative study. International Journal of Mental Health Nursing, 30(5), 1080–1092. https://doi.org/10.1111/inm.12858

Rochette, C., Mériade, L., & Cassière, F. (2023). A grounded theory-based qualitative approach for examining local implementation of public health policies during crises. MethodsX, 11, 102439. https://doi.org/10.1016/j.mex.2023.102439

Rollins, A. L., Eliacin, J., Russ-Jara, A. L., Monroe-Devita, M., Wasmuth, S., Flanagan, M. E., & Salyers, M. P. (2021). Organizational conditions that influence work engagement and burnout: A qualitative study of mental health workers. Psychiatric Rehabilitation Journal, 44(3), 229. https://psycnet.apa.org/doi/10.1037/prj0000472

Rose, G., & Smith, L. (2018). Mental health recovery, goal setting and working alliance in an Australian community-managed organization. Health Psychology Open, 5(1), 2055102918774674. https://doi.org/10.1177/2055102918774674

Rossi, R., Socci, V., Pacitti, F., Di Lorenzo, G., Di Marco, A., Siracusano, A., & Rossi, A. (2020). Mental health outcomes among frontline and second-line health care workers during Italy's Coronavirus disease 2019 (COVID-19) Pandemic. JAMA Network Open, 3(5), e2010185. https://doi.org/10.1001/jamanetworkopen.2020.10185

Roth-Cohen, O., Levy, S., & Zigdon, A. (2021). The mediated role of credibility on information sources and patient awareness toward patient rights. International Journal of Environmental Research and Public Health, 18(16), 8628. https://doi.org/10.3390/ijerph18168628

Rudolph, J. E., Zhong, Y., Duggal, P., Mehta, S. H., & Lau, B. (2023). Defining representativeness of study samples in medical and population health research. BMJ Medicine, 2(1), e000399. https://doi.org/10.1136/bmjmed-2022-000399

Salari, N., Khazaie, H., Hosseinian-Far, A., Khaledi-Paveh, B., Kazeminia, M., Mohammadi, M., Shohaimi, S., Daneshkhah, A., & Eskandari, S. (2020). The prevalence of stress, anxiety, and depression within front-line healthcare workers caring for COVID-19 patients: A systematic review and meta-regression. Human Resources for Health, 18(1), 100. https://doi.org/10.1186/s12960-020-00544-1

Sampson, M., Melnyk, B. M., & Hoying, J. (2019). Intervention effects of the mindbodystrong cognitive behavioral skills building program on newly licensed registered nurses' mental health, healthy lifestyle behaviors, and job satisfaction. JONA: The Journal of Nursing Administration, 49(10), 487. https://doi.org/10.1097/NNA.0000000000000792

Sánchez-Guardiola Paredes, C., Aguaded Ramírez, E. M., & Rodríguez-Sabiote, C. (2021). Content validation of a semi-structured interview to analyze the management of suffering. International Journal of Environmental Research and Public Health, 18(21), 11393. https://doi.org/10.3390/ijerph182111393

Scanlan, J. N., & Still, M. (2019). Relationships between burnout, turnover intention, job satisfaction, job demands, and job resources for mental health personnel in an Australian mental health service. BMC Health Services Research, 19(1), 62. https://doi.org/10.1186/s12913-018-3841-z

Scheepers, R. A., Emke, H., Epstein, R. M., & Lombarts, K. M. J. M. H. (2020). The impact of mindfulness-based interventions on doctors' well-being and performance: A systematic review. Medical Education, 54(2), 138–149. https://doi.org/10.1111/medu.14020

Scheffelaar, A., Janssen, M., & Luijkx, K. (2021). The story as a quality instrument: Developing an instrument for quality improvement based on narratives of older adults receiving long-term care. International Journal of Environmental Research and Public Health, 18(5), 2773. https://doi.org/10.3390/ijerph18052773

Scheunemann, A., Kim, A. W., Moolla, A., & Subramaney, U. (2023). Public psychiatric healthcare workers employed coping strategies during the COVID-19 pandemic in southern Gauteng, South Africa. PLoS One, 18(8), e0277392. https://doi.org/10.1371/journal.pone.0277392

Secapramana, L. V. H., Hariyanto, V., & Anggoro, S. (2020). Employee assistance program as the supporting system of quality of work life to cope with occupational stress. Journal of Educational, Health and Community Psychology, 9(2), 97-115.

Semyonov-Tal, K., & Lewin-Epstein, N. (2021). The importance of combining open-ended and closed-ended questions when conducting patient satisfaction surveys in hospitals. Health Policy Open, 2, 100033. https://doi.org/10.1016/j.hpopen.2021.100033

Settineri, S., Frisone, F., Alibrandi, A., & Merlo, E. M. (2019). Emotional suppression and oneiric expression in psychosomatic disorders: Early manifestations in emerging adulthood and young patients. Frontiers in Psychology, 10. https://www.frontiersin.org/articles/10.3389/fpsyg.2019.01897

Shah, A. H., Becene, I. A., Nguyen, K. T. N. H., Stuart, J. J., West, M. G., Berrill,

J. E., Hankins, J., Borba, C. P., & Rich-Edwards, J. W. (2022). A qualitative analysis of psychosocial stressors and health impacts of the COVID-19 pandemic on frontline healthcare personnel in the United States. SSM. Qualitative Research in Health, 2, 100130. https://doi.org/10.1016/j.ssmqr. 2022.100130

Shalaby, R. A. H., & Agyapong, V. I. O. (2020). Peer support in mental Health: Literature review. JMIR Mental Health, 7(6), e15572. https://doi.org/10. 2196/15572

Shenoi, A. N., Kalyanaraman, M., Pillai, A., Raghava, P. S., & Day, S. (2018). Burnout and psychological distress among pediatric critical care physicians in the United States. Critical Care Medicine, 46(1), 116. https://doi.org/10. 1097/CCM.0000000000002751

Shimi, J., & Manwaring, G. (2017). The resilient graduate. InGraduate attributes in higher education (pp. 58-79). Routledge.

Shorey, S., & Ng, E. D. (2022). Examining characteristics of descriptive phenomenological nursing studies: A scoping review. Journal of Advanced Nursing, 78(7), 1968–1979. https://doi.org/10.1111/jan.15244

Siedlecki, S. L. (2020). Understanding descriptive research designs and methods. Clinical Nurse Specialist, 34(1), 8–12. https://doi.org/10.1097/NUR. 0000000000000493

Smajic, E., Avdic, D., Pasic, A., Prcic, A., & Stancic, M. (2022). Mixed methodology of scientific research in healthcare. Journal of the Society for Medical Informatics of Bosnia & Herzegovina, 30(1), 57–60. https://doi.org/ 10.5455/aim.2022.30.57-60

Sukhera, J. (2022). Narrative reviews: Flexible, rigorous, and practical. Journal of Graduate Medical Education, 14(4), 414–417. https://doi.org/10.4300/ JGME-D-22-00480.1

Sun, J., Sun, R., Jiang, Y., Chen, X., Li, Z., Ma, Z., Wei, J., He, C., & Zhang, L. (2020). The relationship between psychological health and social support: Evidence from physicians in China. PLoS One, 15(1), e0228152. https:// doi.org/10.1371/journal.pone.0228152

Tahara, M., Mashizume, Y., & Takahashi, K. (2021). Coping mechanisms: Exploring strategies Japanese healthcare workers utilize to reduce stress and improve mental health during the COVID-19 Pandemic. International Journal of Environmental Research and Public Health, 18(1), Article 1. https://doi.org/10.3390/ijerph18010131

Talaee, N., Varahram, M., Jamaati, H., Salimi, A., Attarchi, M., Kazempour Dizaji, M., & Seyedmehdi, S. M. (2020). Stress and burnout in health care workers during COVID-19 pandemic: validation of a questionnaire. Journal of Public Health, 1-6. https://doi.org/10.1007/s10389-020-01313-z

Taylor, A. K., Armitage, S., & Kausar, A. (2021). A challenge in qualitative research: Family members sitting in on interviews about sensitive subjects. Health Expectations: An International Journal of Public Participation in Health Care and Health Policy, 24(4), 1545–1546. https://doi.org/10.1111/hex.13263

Taylor, S. E., & Stanton, A. L. (2007). Coping resources, coping processes, and mental health. Annual Review of Clinical Psychology, 3, 377–401. https://doi.org/10.1146/annurev.clinpsy.3.022806.091520

Tenny, S., Brannan, J. M., & Brannan, G. D. (2022). Qualitative study. StatPearls Publishing.

Terry, L., & Newham, R. (2020). Understanding and applying personality types in healthcare communication. Nursing Standard, 35(7), 27–34. https://doi.org/10.7748/ns.2020.e11490

Thomas, S. P., & Sohn, B. K. (2023). From uncomfortable squirm to self-discovery: A phenomenological analysis of the bracketing experience. International Journal of Qualitative Methods, 22. https://doi.org/10.1177/16094069231191635

Trezona, A., Dodson, S., Fitzsimon, E., LaMontagne, A. D., & Osborne, R. H. (2020). Field-testing and refinement of the organisational health literacy responsiveness self-assessment (Org-HLR) tool and process. International Journal of Environmental Research and Public Health, 17(3), 1000. https://doi.org/10.3390/ijerph17031000

Tsaras, K., Daglas, A., Mitsi, D., Papathanasiou, I. V., Tzavella, F., Zyga, S., & Fradelos, E. C. (2018). A cross-sectional study for the impact of coping strategies on mental health disorders among psychiatric nurses. Health Psychology Research, 6(1), 7466. https://doi.org/10.4081/hpr.2018.7466

U.S. Bureau of Labor Statistics. (2023).Healthcare occupations: Characteristics of the employed. U.S. Bureau of Labor Statistics. https://www.bls.gov/spotlight/2023/healthcare-occupations-in-2022/home.htm

Vahedi, S., Gargari, R., & Gholami, S. (2016). Effect of the Penn Resiliency Program on students with emotional problems. International Journal of Educational and Psychological Researches, 2.https://doi.org/10.4103/2395-2296.180302

Vamvakas, E., Kontogeorgou, I., Ntaountaki, A., Karkouli, G., Pisimisi, E., Karampekiou, E., Politis, E., Moskofi, I., Konitopoulos, D., Dokoutsidou, E., Grigoropoulou, M., Theodorakopoulou, M., & Armaganidis, A. (2022). Occupational stress and quality of life among health professionals during the COVID-19 pandemic. Journal of Critical Care Medicine, 8(3), 182–192. https://doi.org/10.2478/jccm-2022-0012

Van Hees, S. G. M., Carlier, B. E., Blonk, R. W. B., & Oomens, S. (2022). Strengthening supervisor support for employees with common mental health problems: Developing a workplace intervention using intervention mapping. BMC Public Health, 22(1), 1146. https://doi.org/10.1186/s12889-022-13545-7

Vasileiou, K., Barnett, J., Thorpe, S., & Young, T. (2018). Characterising and justifying sample size sufficiency in interview-based studies: Systematic analysis of qualitative health research over a 15-year period. BMC Medical Research Methodology, 18(1), 148. https://doi.org/10.1186/s12874-018-0594-7

Wasti, S. P., Simkhada, P., van Teijlingen, E. R., Sathian, B., & Banerjee, I. (2022). The growing importance of mixed-methods research in health. Nepal Journal of Epidemiology, 12(1), 1175–1178. https://doi.org/10.3126/nje.v12i1.43633

Weiner, L., Berna, F., Nourry, N., Severac, F., Vidailhet, P., & Mengin, A. C. (2020). Efficacy of an online cognitive behavioral therapy program developed for healthcare workers during the COVID-19 pandemic: The REduction of STress (REST) study protocol for a randomized controlled trial. Trials, 21(1), 870. https://doi.org/10.1186/s13063-020-04772-7

Wilson, C. A., Metwally, H., Heavner, S., Kennedy, A. B., & Britt, T. W. (2022). Chronicling moral distress among healthcare providers during the COVID-19 pandemic: A longitudinal analysis of mental health strain, burnout, and maladaptive coping behaviors. International Journal of Mental Health Nursing, 31(1), 111–127. https://doi.org/10.1111/inm.12942

Wooyoung Kim, A., Maaroganye, K., & Subramaney, U. (2021). Mental health experiences of public psychiatric healthcare workers during COVID-19 across southern Gauteng, South Africa: A call for strengthening. South African Health Review, (1), 143–151.

Wu, Y., Shao, J., Zhang, D., Wang, Y., Wang, S., Wang, Z., Qu, Y., & Gu, J. (2022). Pathways from self-disclosure to medical coping strategy among adolescents with moderate and major depression during the COVID-19 pandemic: A mediation of self-efficacy. Frontiers in Psychiatry, 13.https://www.frontiersin.org/articles/10.3389/fpsyt.2022.976386

Wu, Y., Yu, W., Wu, X., Wan, H., Wang, Y., & Lu, G. (2020). Psychological resilience and positive coping styles among Chinese undergraduate students: A cross-sectional study. BMC Psychology, 8(1), 79. https://doi.org/10.1186/s40359-020-00444-y

Yang, Y., & Hayes, J. A. (2020). Causes and consequences of burnout among mental health professionals: A practice-oriented review of recent empirical literature. Psychotherapy, 57(3), 426–436. https://doi.org/10.1037/pst0000317

Yarborough, M. (2021). Moving towards less biased research. BMJ Open Science, 5(1), e100116. https://doi.org/10.1136/bmjos-2020-100116

Yıldırım, M., Arslan, G., & Özaslan, A. (2020). Perceived risk and mental health problems among healthcare professionals during COVID-19 pandemic: Exploring the mediating effects of resilience and coronavirus fear. International Journal of Mental Health and Addiction, 1-11. https://doi.org/10.1007/s11469-020-00424-8

Yu, J., Park, J., & Hyun, S. S. (2021). Impacts of the COVID-19 pandemic on employees' work stress, well-being, mental health, organizational citizenship behavior, and employee-customer identification. Journal of Hospitality Marketing & Management, 30(5), 529–548. https://doi.org/10.1080/19368623.2021.1867283

Zhang, B., Li, H., Jin, X., Peng, W., Wong, C. L., & Qiu, D. (2022). Prevalence and factors associated with compassion satisfaction and compassion fatigue among Chinese oncology healthcare professionals: A cross-sectional survey. Asia-Pacific Journal of Oncology Nursing, 9(3), 153–160. https://doi.org/10.1016/j.apjon.2021.12.012